"A masterful and comprehensive approach to leading and managing transformation efforts of any type or size."

—PHIL LENIR, Co-founder and President, CoachingOurselves

"Bev has created a framework that will revolutionize the way you as a leader create alignment, engage others, manage resistance, and implement the culture shifts you need for systemic change."

—JEAN WEST, Director of Mental Health, York Support Services Network; and Professional Certified Coach

"I encourage anyone who wants to effect positive change to read this book—and reference it time and time again as you use Bev's process and tools."

—PAUL SLAGGERT, retired Director, Stayer Center for Executive Education, University of Notre Dame

"Compelling and powerful! This is not just a good read, but a challenge to shift our notions of what it means to bring meaningful change in a digital world where new trends are reshaping our workplaces, society, and the very cultures we live in."

—DR. RAYE KASS, Professor of Applied Human Sciences, Concordia University

Beverley Patwell

Leading Meaningful Change

Capturing the Hearts, Minds, and Souls of the People You Lead, Work With, and Serve

Vancouver / Berkeley

To Don, who captured my heart
and brings meaning to my life;
and in memory of my mother, Lucy,
and my mentors,
Charlie and Edie Seashore.

Contents

Introduction

Leading Meaningful Change is for leaders, managers, and anyone who is interested in or already leading and managing a short change, a transition, and/or a larger transformation (I use the word "change" throughout the book when the concept cuts through all three levels).

The book provides a complete framework of principles and a four-stage process to help you go beyond developing plans and tactics to lead and implement changes in processes, technology, policies, procedures, and organizational culture. In going beyond, I show you how to create and participate in change experiences that capture the hearts, minds, and souls of the people you lead, work with, and serve. The Leading Meaningful Change (abbreviated henceforth as LMC) Framework and Process are human and engaging and will motivate your organization and community to work together toward a higher purpose and achieve results that are greater than any single person's contribution.

The feature character in LMC is You and your Use-of-Self. In this regard, this book is a sequel to *Triple Impact Coaching: Use-of-Self in the Coaching Process* (2006), which I wrote with Edith Whitfield Seashore, one of the luminaries in the field of organizational development and my mentor. The book in your hands elaborates on the evolution and continued importance of mastering Use-of-Self as a key leadership competency in today's hyper-connected world. This book will help you reflect on and master your Use-of-Self as you lead and manage teams, work in networks of teams, and collaborate and partner with others to make a positive impact in your organization, in your community, and on this planet.

Over my years of consulting and teaching, I have learned that a meaningful change journey is not static. It is a dynamic and continuous learning process that ebbs and flows depending on one's relationships and interactions with the people involved in or impacted by the change process. At the core of the change process is the Use-of-Self. It is the only thing you can control.

In this book, you will explore the roots of and the inspirations that have influenced and matured the Use-of-Self foundation for leading meaningful change. The original keys to Use-of-Self—feedback, choices, reframing, and power—will be revisited and updated to be more responsive to today's complex world, digital workplace, social media, and virtual working relationships. I provide real-life examples and advice from leaders and managers who have successfully applied these keys in their face-to-face and virtual interactions and in how they have learned to develop others to lead meaningful change.

→ Why Capture Hearts, Minds, and Souls?

The distinctive word in my book title, *Leading Meaningful Change*, is "meaningful." There is a clear reason for this. People generally do not like or accept change that is done to them without their participating in the planning for it, having prior knowledge of it, or being asked for their consent that the change will improve their situation. People are most engaged when they are involved in the change process. That is when the change becomes meaningful for them and they know they can make a difference.

I came to recognize the power of the phrase "capturing the hearts, minds, and souls of the people" when I was working with the senior management team at the City of Ottawa (a case study that I will discuss in chapter 7). I asked each member of the team, "What does leading meaningful change mean to you?" Consistent in all of my interviews was some type of reference to the change process having a "magic sauce"—an inner motivation that occurs when people are inspired to be part of the change. The Ottawa city leaders shared with their teams the purpose, vision, and values that would guide the change journey they would all take together. They created a plan that had meaning for people. This sentiment was captured in a single phrase by the city manager, Steve Kanellakos, who said, "When you are successful leading meaningful change, it means that you have captured the hearts and souls of the people. They believe in a higher purpose, something greater than their own single contribution."

Why must we be concerned about the hearts and souls of people and not just their minds? I believe the answer is increasingly evident. People want and can easily seek connection with others. They are craving meaning in their jobs, better work/life balance, and more shared power. They are concerned about improving society and ensuring the health of the planet. For some people, the word "soul" has a spiritual connotation that calls on them to make a positive difference in the world, working toward a higher purpose. For others, "soul" evokes a strong emotional reaction that reminds them to treat people as human beings, not just as employees, clients, or subjects in the change process. Having soul is a reminder that we are not alone. We are connected to each other and part of a larger community, society, or universe. When we lead change, we must work for the benefit of everyone.

→ What Is Meaningful Change?

The key to leading change that appeals to hearts, minds, and souls is to make the change meaningful. How do I define this? In my view, meaningful change

- is based on a shared purpose that compels people to want to be engaged and involved throughout the journey;

- is a continuous learning and development process that takes place at all levels: individual, team, organization, community, and planet;

- reduces resistance to change and improves performance at the individual, team, and organizational levels;

- is effective in helping people lead, manage, participate in, and evaluate the human side of the change and culture shifts;

- pays attention to the most important instrument in your toolkit, your own Use-of-Self, by helping you become more intentional about how you show up, the choices you make, and the impact you have on others and your work; and

- builds and leverages teamwork and collaboration across the organization and externally with partners, influencers, and decision makers, which leads to better, more sustainable business solutions and results that are far greater than what one person or group could achieve on their own.

In this book, you will learn about the LMC Framework, composed of seven principles, and the LMC Process based on four stages—alignment, integration, action, and renewal—to ensure any change effort, no matter how complex or large, is effective and successful. You will hear from leaders and managers who share their stories, experiences, and favorite tools that helped them capture the hearts, minds, and souls of people they lead, work with, and serve. LMC is a journey that calls us to take care of and pay attention to all souls on board, including our own.

→ Organization of the Book

The book is divided into two parts.

Part 1: The Leading Meaningful Change Journey
Part 1 of the book presents the elements of the LMC journey over seven chapters, including a detailed case study.

Chapter 1: The Main Character in Leading Meaningful Change Is You: *Use-of-Self in the Change Process*
This chapter discusses the single most critical element and the main character in leading meaningful change: your Use-of-Self. This chapter will

- explain the original roots of Use-of-Self in the change process;
- discuss three studies that shaped the evolution of a new vision of Use-of-Self and the LMC Framework; and
- present the new Use-of-Self 2.0, which is the foundation for this book.

Chapter 2: Six Keys to Guide Your Use-of-Self in the Leading Meaningful Change Process
Developing Use-of-Self is a lifelong learning process. This chapter will explain the six keys to guide your Use-of-Self in the LMC Process, with examples and exercises to help you lead meaningful change. The six keys are:

- Being aware of and accountable for our choices
- Cultivating Use-of-Self as an instrument of change

- Reframing
- Navigating the dynamics of power
- Giving and receiving feedback
- Appreciating and leveraging our diversity

Chapter 3: The Leading Meaningful Change Framework
This chapter begins by explaining the seven principles of the LMC Framework that form the foundation of any change journey. These principles are necessary to guide leaders through the LMC Process. They are:

- Create a shared purpose, vision, principles, and values.
- Develop and engage people.
- Build relationships and foster teamwork and collaboration.
- Develop the plan to align with strategic priorities and goals.
- Develop a unified organizational culture to support change.
- Set up systems, structures, and processes to support the change.
- Conduct a continuous evaluation of the plan, actions, and impacts.

Chapter 4: The Four Stages of the Leading Meaningful Change Process
In this chapter, I explain the LMC Process that I created and use in my work, consisting of four stages to guide you through a change journey. This process is multifaceted and comprehensive, ensuring that you can lead and manage meaningful change and your Use-of-Self throughout the entire journey.

Also in this chapter, I present tools to evaluate each stage of the LMC Process, the Change Leadership Challenge Exercise, and the Master Change Plan template that you can use to map your change journey.

Chapter 5: Maximizing the Power of Teams
Teamwork is an essential ingredient to achieve the goals of your change effort using the LMC Framework and Process. We will explore the challenges and complexities of building cohesive teams. I will also define ten guidelines for the formation and operation of cohesive teams. A case example illustrates the concepts.

Chapter 6: Tools to Foster Teamwork, Collaboration, and Partnerships in Leading Meaningful Change
This chapter will delve into a number of specific activities that I use to foster teamwork, collaboration, and partnerships. Exercises are provided along with two case examples of how a university dean and a not-for-profit community theater director used the concepts of this book to leverage the power of teams as they led meaningful change efforts in their organizations.

Chapter 7: Case Study: City of Ottawa—One City, One Team
As the new city manager at the City of Ottawa, Steve Kanellakos was tasked with improving the delivery of city services and creating long-term sustainability throughout the corporation. Based on his previous experience and tenure with the city, he knew that he needed a plan to transition to his new role and build a cohesive senior leadership team. Together they developed a strategy to lead this meaningful change that went beyond tactics to capture the hearts and souls of the people they led, worked with, and served.

This chapter is a case study covering this leadership team's journey through the first two years (2016 to 2018) of leading a city-wide transition and culture shift to adopt the mindset, values, and behaviors of "Servant Leadership" as the new guide to their day-to-day work. It provides the background and context for this change, a summary of their approach through the lens of the LMC Process, and an overview of how they created a cohesive leadership team that inspired people across the corporation to embrace the shared purpose they called "One City, One Team" and achieve results that were far greater than any single contribution could produce.

Part 2: The Leading Meaningful Change Toolkit

The toolkit is designed to help you put into practice the concepts presented in part 1. Please customize and adapt them to reflect your context and advance your work to lead meaningful change. This toolkit lists the exercises covered in each chapter, plus provides ten additional exercises that you can do as you go about any change in your organization.

→ The LMC Framework and Process Are Forward-Thinking

Leading Meaningful Change is based on my observations and work over more than two decades with numerous change leaders and managers who worked on large-scale and complex organizational changes. The LMC Framework and Process presented in this book are based on three studies that focused on change leadership. This research confirmed that the concept of Use-of-Self has endured over time and continues to play an important role in leading meaningful change.

But the research also revealed that we need to go beyond plans and tactics to create meaning for people throughout any change journey and take into account the new trends that are reshaping our workplaces, society, and cultures across the planet. These trends are moving us to become more attentive to our human needs, including the need to

- foster cultures of trust and accountability;
- create healthy workplaces where people can thrive;
- create stronger alignment between business and key political stakeholders on a vision and path forward to improve the world;

- respect the diversity of people, cultures, and our work/life environments;

- build and leverage teamwork, especially when working in multidisciplinary and cross-professional teams and networks;

- mentor people and develop their talents, skills, and competencies for the future;

- communicate clearly and have difficult conversations when a message is not popular or perceived as positive yet requires the support of the audience and other stakeholders;

- innovate and be prepared to deal with the impact of disruptive changes from artificial intelligence and new technologies; and

- teach people how to accept the new constant of change.

Leading Meaningful Change is responsive to these trends. It incorporates new concepts, tools, and approaches to help you validate your work, celebrate your successes, and develop strategies to address your current challenges and future change journeys.

PART 1

The
Leading
Meaningful
Change
Journey

The Main Character in Leading Meaningful Change Is *You*: Use-of-Self in the Change Process

In the late 1990s, coaching was just starting to surface as a support for leadership development, and in some cases was even formalized inside organizations. Working with my mentor and colleague Edith Whitfield Seashore, we developed a coaching model we called Triple Impact Coaching (TIC) and spelled it out in our book *Triple Impact Coaching: Use-of-Self in the Coaching Process* (2006). Our model was originally designed for a specific group of research and development managers who were leading the integration of two teams—product support and new product introduction—into one. Our TIC model was successful and has since been adapted and used globally with leaders and managers in all types and sizes of businesses and industries in the public, private, and plural sectors (the last comprising our communities, charities, not-for-profits, clubs, etc.).

At the core of the TIC model is the concept called Use-of-Self. This concept continues to sit at the core of the new LMC Framework that this book presents. It forms the foundation for the seven guiding principles of the LMC Framework that you will learn about in chapter 3. You may be familiar with it already from prior workshops you have taken or articles you have read—or it may be brand new to you. Whatever your background with it, it is worthwhile reading this chapter closely, as the Use-of-Self model I present here has evolved since the publication of our book and has been enhanced with research and examples that reflect the current trends and challenges we face in our workplaces and our world.

→ The Roots of Use-of-Self

My introduction to Use-of-Self goes back to the work and teachings of two luminaries in the field of organizational development, the late Dr. Charles Seashore and his wife, Edith Whitfield Seashore (Charlie and Edie, as they liked to be called). I met Charlie in 1995 when he taught in the Master of Applied Social Science program (now called Applied Human Sciences) at Concordia University in Montreal, Quebec, Canada. At the time, this was a new Master of Arts program in organizational development, modeled after American University's Master of Science in Organizational Development, where both Charlie and Edie also taught.

I was a student in the first graduating cohort. In that program, we were provided with a unique opportunity to select one elective course for our second year. One day over lunch, Charlie talked about Edie's course, "Use-of-Self as Instrument," which sounded interesting, so I chose it as my elective. This course changed my life, as it did for many others in our class. Edie and I connected right away and developed a relationship that flourished. She became not just my teacher but my mentor, coach, business partner, and close friend.

In 2000, Edie agreed to work with one of my client organizations, where I had been hired to deliver a coaching program to develop leaders and teams to lead and manage change. When we got together to do the teaching handover, I presented Edie with a binder of materials I had created for this client. She read them over and encouraged me to write a book about the TIC concept and the Use-of-Self. I agreed, but only on the condition that we author it together. This was the start of a mutually rewarding and long friendship that lasted until her death in 2013. In addition to teaching together at McGill University and working with our clients in Canada, we published our book, which continues to influence many coaching programs throughout the world and is the foundation for my coaching and organizational development practice and research today.

What exactly is Use-of-Self? What did the Seashores mean by it? In a special edition of the *Organizational Development Journal*, their daughters, Becky May and Kim Seashore, wrote:

> Our parents exemplified the integration of Use-of-Self beyond the buzzword, beyond a concept that needed to be isolated or highlighted, beyond a tool exclusively of or for the trade of (OD). One of our mother's favorite sayings was: "A master in the art of living draws no sharp distinction between his work and his play, his labor and his leisure, his mind and his body, his education and his recreation. He hardly knows which is which. He simply pursues his vision of excellence through whatever he is doing and leaves others to determine whether he is working or playing. To himself he always seems to be doing both. Enough for him that he does it well."[1]

Edie and Charlie lived this motto and philosophy of the integrated self. They may not have created the phrase or concept "Use-of-Self," but they now have a legacy that lives on.[2]

Another passage that Charlie wrote in the foreword of *Triple Impact Coaching* sums up superbly the meaning of Use-of-Self:

> The focus of Triple Impact Coaching is *Use-of-Self*. It is simple, profound and infinitely complex—all at the same time.... We know the value of instruments and tools of the trade in all of our various professions. We also know that there is a temptation to attribute the success of our work

to the technical tools or strategies that we use and the accompanying belief that all we need to do to increase our range of effectiveness is to acquire more of these tools.

The simple theme to pay the most attention to is the person using the tools, meaning oneself, rather than focusing on the design of the tool. An excellent tool in the hands of a struggling professional can do great damage while an imperfect tool in the hands of a true craftsperson can morph into an awesome impact at individual, team and organizational levels.[3]

Charlie elaborated on the deeper philosophy and psychology embedded in Use-of-Self as a core leadership tool in an article he later published with colleagues, entitled "Doing Good by Knowing Who You Are: The Instrumental Self as an Agent of Change":

Use-of-Self is a link between our personal potential and the world of change. It starts with our understanding of who we are, our conscious perception of our Self, commonly called the ego, and the unconscious or out of awareness part of our Self that is always along for the ride, and on many occasions is actually the driver. This understanding of Self is then linked with our perceptions of what is needed in the world around us and our choice of a strategy, and a role in which to use our energy to create change. Our focus here is on the potential for changing one's own world—the world as we perceive it, and to act on it and leave our mark and legacy for others to appreciate.[4]

In their article "Use-of-Self: Presence with the Power to Transform Systems," Mary Ann Rainey and Brenda B. Jones, both colleagues of the Seashores, expanded on the Use-of-Self concept as it applies to change agents described as leaders, managers, consultants, and professionals at the forefront of change. They state that transformational

Table 1 Four Elements of Self as Perceived by Mary Ann Rainey and Brenda B. Jones

Self-Awareness	Self-Concept
Level of knowledge about self (e.g., values, biases, tendencies, culture, and the extent that knowledge is applied consistently in everyday life).	Self-perception. The broader collection of assumptions and beliefs one holds about one's self. Who am I to me?
Extent to which I am self-aware.	*Three words I use to describe me.*
Self-Esteem	**Social-Self**
Value placed on one's self-concept. Overall evaluation and judgment of one's worth, usually viewed against one's judgment of others.	Relatability. Awareness of and healthy interaction with others. Ability to establish and manage quality relationships.
My level of self-esteem.	*How I rate my social-self.*

Coaching versus Mentoring

This chapter is largely about Use-of-Self as it pertains to coaching. It also plays a role in mentoring situations, though other factors are also required. For clarity, here is the distinction I make between coaching and mentoring. While I believe all leaders have a responsibility to coach and develop people to be effective in their roles, not all leaders mentor. Table 2 shows how the two differ.

Some organizations use a hybrid or blended model that combines both coaching and mentoring. But for purposes of LMC, keep these distinctions in mind as we discuss coaching and mentoring.

Table 2 **Coaching versus Mentoring**

Coaching	Mentoring
Short-term development	Long-term development
Performance-driven: Setting goals, taking action, monitoring, evaluating, and sustaining change over time	Vision-driven: Exchanging wisdom, support, learning, and guidance to achieve vision, purpose, and strategic priorities
Technical or professional focus: Role, function, or service	Political, professional, and/or technical focus: Guidance on navigating the organizational context, people, networks, and community
Professional relationship between coach and employee: Usually formal	Privileged relationship between mentor and mentee: Can be formal or informal
Inspires respect for competence: Skills, knowledge, and expertise	Is a role model: Values, beliefs, mindset, and behaviors

change begins with the change agent through a process that involves understanding self, thoughtful Use-of-Self, and engaging with a presence that motivates, inspires, and engenders followership. They believe that when these agents of change transform their capabilities, including their emotional intelligence, they also transform the capabilities of the system in which they live and work. They developed the framework shown in Table 1 to help analyze the self in a matrix of four dimensions: self-awareness, self-concept, self-esteem, and social-self.[5]

Based on these roots, you can see that Use-of-Self goes beyond just self-awareness to being a fully integrated way of living and being. It is a mindset, philosophy, and process that needs to be attended to and developed throughout the change and transformation process. In this context of change, Use-of-Self can be challenging, as you may be leading and managing others while you, yourself, are going through change and uncertainty. For these reasons, the Use-of-Self remains the core concept in the LMC Framework just as it was in the TIC model.

Our Use-of-Self is in constant play in many situations in organizational learning and development. As leaders and change agents, we coach and mentor others and we are often coached and mentored ourselves. I believe coaching and mentoring are essential skills and provide valuable support for development, especially when we take on, transition to, or prepare for new roles, assignments, or opportunities. Use-of-Self therefore is essential for supporting the growing trends of multiple generations of employees working together in one workplace, the increase need for reverse coaching and upward mentoring whereby the younger generation coaches and mentors their more senior colleagues.

Use-of-Self also applies when we learn new processes and technologies. It is especially important when we need to develop skills to navigate the political networks within and outside of the organization.

→ **How Use-of-Self Creates a Triple Impact**

When Edie and I first published our book *Triple Impact Coaching*, we devised the diagram shown in Figure 1 to visualize the process implied in the term "Triple Impact Coaching." The diagram pictures a series of concentric circles reflecting the three layers that make up organizations: individuals, teams, and the entire organization. At the center of the diagram is a bifurcated circle, with "Aware" on one side and "Unaware" on the other. A needle called "Self" cuts across the dial, suggesting how Use-of-Self turns the consciousness of each person and layer of the organization from being unaware to being aware. At the left side are the four keys—choices, reframing, power, and feedback—necessary to master and turn the needle.

Our thinking was that the greater the awareness and efficacy of each leader's Use-of-Self, the more informed, intentional, and conscious individuals, teams, and the entire organization will be about the choices they make in their approach to achieving the desired performance. As one moves toward awareness, it has an impact on one's team, and then on the organization. Individual, team, organization: hence the name *Triple* Impact Coaching.

One of the global thought leaders in the field of management, Dr. Henry Mintzberg, Cleghorn Professor at McGill University, redefined the role of the manager in his book *Managing*. He describes the manager as someone who manages on three planes: through information, with people, and for action (Figure 2).[6]

This model shows the manager sitting in the middle, between the unit they manage and the world outside— the rest of the organization as well as what is around the organization. Two roles for a manager exist on each plane. On the information plane, managers communicate (all around) and control (inside). On the people plane, they lead (inside) and link (to the outside). On the action plane, managers do or act (inside) and deal (with the outside). Managers work on all three planes to frame (conceive

Figure 1 **The Original TIC Model**

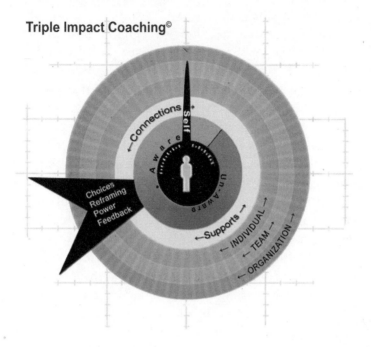

Figure 2 **Mintzberg Model of Managing**

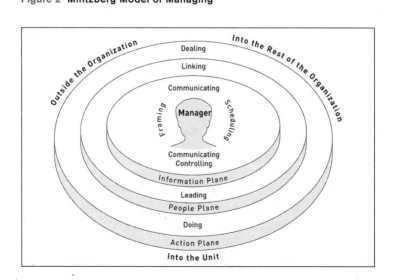

strategies, establish priorities) and schedule work (including their own time).

Mintzberg states that the overriding purpose of managing is to ensure that the unit serves its basic purpose, whether it is to sell products in a retail chain, care for the elderly in a nursing home, or whatever it may be. This requires taking action by coaching, motivating, building teams, strengthening culture, and other key steps. To do this, managers use information to coach other people to take action, such as setting a target for a sales team, sharing information about a customer, etc.

For Mintzberg, coaching thus plays a critical role in the development and effectiveness of leaders and managers. They must learn how to coach others, but equally important, they must learn how to be coached themselves for success. Accordingly, it is impossible to look at the interplay of leadership and coaching without reflecting on the Use-of-Self and vice versa. Coaching is an integral role of leading and managing in the workplace and is an essential skill for everyone in the organization.

Since the publication of *Triple Impact Coaching*, I have been using the model in my consulting work with scores of organizations to help them achieve meaningful change. Throughout the course of this book, you will read about several of these organizations and how they implemented the elements of Use-of-Self across their entire leadership and management teams to achieve triple impact. My clients tell me that when they pay attention to their Use-of-Self, they are more self-aware, intentional, and authentic in how they are and want to be "showing up" in their relationships at work, at home, as members of their communities, and on this planet. When they trust themselves, they are able to trust others, which leads to better ways of working with people and faster paths to reaching common ground, collaborating as teams, and achieving their desired organizational goals. When the Use-of-Self mindset, principles, and practices are applied, leaders report achievements that are far greater than their single contribution.

→ Evolving Use-of-Self for Today's World

Before I review the skills that help leaders and managers learn and master Use-of-Self, I want to stress that my original concepts of Use-of-Self have evolved over the past decade. No model in organizational development can remain static in this fast-changing world. Since our book was first published in 2006, technology especially has transformed the way we live, work, and play. When TIC was developed, we were still storing data on floppy disks and flash drives, and using iPods and DVDs to listen to our music and watch videos and movies. Most of us had BlackBerries, Motorola flip phones, and desktop computers. Today, people are plugged-in all the time and have instant access to data and information. Instead of six degrees of separation, we are only one click away from any individual, group, or society.

Add to this the fact that in most organizations, multiple generations are working together and whose education, values, experiences, and instincts are far different than the baby boomers who occupied most senior positions in the early 2000s. In many organizations, millennials are now the managers, if not senior leaders, as boomers retire. Those boomers who are still working are not always the most technologically savvy.

As a result of these transformational changes, it is no surprise that the application of Use-of-Self had to change. On the technology side, the skills that leaders need to have must extend beyond face-to-face interactions. Managers and leaders need to consider how to show up online, on social media platforms, through email, and on any other digital media we use to communicate and work with others. They must understand how to lead and coach a highly diverse workforce, composed of people from many cultures, often international, with differing backgrounds, values, and understandings of the way the world works. The pressure to achieve and succeed in a global world adds complexity to many change efforts, as competitors and disrupters work hard to overthrow the existing leaders in every industry.

To better understand how Use-of-Self needed to evolve, I conducted three studies in the past few years:

- *Change Leadership Challenges*, 2014
- *Triple Impact Coaching: Use-of-Self in the Coaching Process: Reflecting on the Past, Present, and Future*, 2018
- *Leading Meaningful Change*, 2018

From these studies, I drew numerous conclusions that have helped me evolve how leaders and managers develop the skills that will lead them to master their Use-of-Self. The former four keys to Use-of-Self have now become six keys. Here's a review of those studies to provide context for what you will learn as you go through this chapter.

Change Leadership Challenges (2014)

This study involved a review of change leadership challenge projects from approximately 2,000 participants in 27 countries and representing all organizational levels (including managers, directors, senior leaders, and project team members) from private, public, and plural sector organizations. As prework, these study participants completed the Change Leadership Challenge Exercise before attending custom client workshops and programs on leading change and transformation at McGill University, Queen's University, Concordia University, and the University of Notre Dame.

The exercise was their initial assessment of a change project they were working on in their organizations. They also had to identify any hot topics that needed to be addressed during the program. Their projects focused mainly on wanting to learn how to lead a change effort, such as an organizational culture shift, a large-scale organization-wide project or initiative, a merger or acquisition, or the design and implementation of new processes, technologies, products, and services in their organizations. The participants came from different organizations and geographies around the world. A review of their responses found some clear trends in the change leadership competencies they wanted to improve, with top priorities being creating alignment, building strong and cohesive teams, managing resistance and culture shifts, and learning change management methods and tools. Especially notable in their comments was a shift in their focus from the technical and structural processes and systems to concerns about leading and improving the performance of their teams.

Taken together, these comments showed that participants recognized that a dysfunctional individual or team could negatively impact the change process. Thus, activities in creating alignment on a shared purpose and priorities, leading and managing the shifts in the organization's culture, and developing effective teams were essential to them.

This study revealed to me an opportunity to make the work of change that one does in TIC more meaningful and sustainable. The TIC model needed to heighten how it aligns and integrates with real work, rather than as an add-on. Teamwork and organizational culture had to be priorities and worked on throughout any development or change process. Through this study, it was also apparent that regardless of one's role or the size and complexity of the change, it is critical to have both change leadership *and* change management to succeed.

Triple Impact Coaching: Use-of-Self in the Coaching Process: Reflecting on the Past, Present, and Future (2018)[7]

This study involved a series of formal conversations I had with colleagues and multigenerational leaders. These people had learned about TIC from my and Edie's book or from workshops or courses they had taken with Edie, me, or others. Participants in the study confirmed that their Use-of-Self was invaluable in their life and work. They described Use-of-Self as a "lens" that helps them see and understand themselves so they can be more aware of their intentions, choices, and the impact they want to have on others.

Using the actual words this group commonly cited to me about Use-of-Self, I constructed a graphic (Figure 3) in the shape of eyeglasses, symbolic of this lens idea. Paradoxically, when I showed some other people this image, they saw in it a pair of handcuffs that, for them, represented how we can often get locked in our own perspectives, stories, and biases that disable, block, or distort our ability to be our "best self." Lastly, this image also represents the infinity symbol, illustrating the Use-of-Self as a complex lifelong journey or the multiplier effect that we can have when leading meaningful change. All three interpretations work.

Figure 3 Word Cloud Based on Survey of Individuals Responding to What Use-of-Self Means to Them

This study revealed that TIC and Use-of-Self needed to move beyond a performance model focused on the individual, team, and organization to become a more continuous, dynamic, and integrated process, which led to the *Leading Meaningful Change* study.

Leading Meaningful Change (2018)

This study included a series of interviews and working sessions with the senior leadership team at the City of Ottawa, where I was working as a consultant helping with the city's transition to a new organizational structure as part of a larger transformation journey. This work took place over two and a half years. The team identified the following key elements as important:

- Hearts and minds
- Vision and a plan
- Organizational culture
- Leadership
- Continuous evaluation

This study helped me evolve the guiding principles of the LMC Framework beyond the foundational ideas of TIC.

→ **The Shift from TIC to LMC**

The results of these three studies, as well as my teaching and consulting work over the last decade, helped me identify several main themes that have driven an effort to evolve TIC into the broader LMC Framework that you will read about in the remainder of this book.

1. *The quest for mastering Use-of-Self applies to all generations and all aspects of life.*
While TIC was not designed as a study on demographics, it became clear that a new framework had to be more explicit in recognizing that the Use-of-Self is a crucial skill to master regardless of one's generation, gender, stage of life, or career field. Use-of-Self is a lifelong learning process and can be applied to all aspects of our lives. It may seem complex and challenging to develop and manage given the fast-paced, turbulent, and constantly changing world that we live and work in, but it is worth mastering.

2. *Use-of-Self is the only element that we can control during change and is the best instrument in our change toolkit.*
TIC was not written with radical change in mind, but it is now clear that the only constant in modern life is change.

A new framework had to incorporate the dynamic of change as inevitable. Nevertheless, regardless of all the changes and complexities we face in our lives, people still want to live their best selves. In the midst of the storm, we still have a choice in what we think, how we feel, and the actions we take to respond and be accountable. The LMC Framework had to help people master Use-of-Self as the only constant they could rely on.

3. People want to make a positive difference in the way they live their life at home and at work, in their communities and on our planet.
The original TIC model was focused on creating and sustaining alignment on a common vision and strategic goals, and evaluating the performance and the actions of the *individual* and *team* to advance the *organization*, thus the triple impact that I defined earlier. In a new model, Use-of-Self can still be focused on these three levels, but it had to go beyond to include the impact of one's work on the community and planet. Growing sensitivity to our universal connectedness and the need to preserve the planet we live on has increased our need for meaningful relationships and work. People today want to belong to an organization that they respect and that demonstrates in its actions the values they share. They want to be part of and work in an organizational culture that fosters health and wellness, contributes positively to their communities, and makes a difference in the daily life of all stakeholders. They also want to be part of a positive movement that results in something meaningful and larger than themselves, and one that does not ruin the planet but sustains it for future generations.

4. Technology has increased the pace of change and our range of choices.
As stated above, TIC was not written with the astonishing advances in technology in mind. But it is inarguable that

technology has transformed the worlds of work and personal life over the past decade and will continue to evolve and present new opportunities through innovation, automation, and planned and disruptive change. The pace of change has accelerated, and with it comes a continuous process of learning and development. Use-of-Self thus requires us to create space for learning and experimenting so that we can become more self-aware of how to adapt to the changes that technology brings.

Technology also plays a new role in how we all communicate in today's world, which has grown to be even more challenging given the pervasiveness of social media, shorter news cycles, and the volume of immediate and easily accessible information, both real and fake. Use-of-Self in this new world must integrate developing strategies to be agile, reduce resistance, build trusting and effective relationships, work with excessive amounts of data, and yet still communicate clearly.

Technology can be used to help or harm. We have a choice in how we use it. Technology provides real-time, instantaneous access to information and data that can inform our decisions, connect us with people and our communities, and enable us to conduct our businesses. Sometimes we must make choices and decisions in nanoseconds. We know immediately if we are liked, disliked, or are polarizing. We have access to information that lets us know how we are doing individually and as an organization. Social media can also be used to test assumptions, provide ideas, and receive feedback in real time.

In a new framework, the reliance on technology and the impact of the digital world present new developmental opportunities for all of us. We need to be conscious of how we choose to use technology. We also need to cut out the noise, eliminate fake news, and focus on validity and facts by working with sound, current data.

5. *There is a need for new virtual social skills.*

All generations in the three studies expressed concern about the influence of technology in their Use-of-Self. People want to seek meaningful relationships and connections, yet the increasing use and abuse of technology make that difficult. With cyberbullying and threats to our personal well-being and security, people must be intentional about setting personal and professional boundaries. They must also protect their psychological safety when they show up online and use social media. They must decide who they want to follow and who they want to influence—or not.

Gen Zs also told us that they learn social skills online that previous generations learned via face-to-face interactions and in small groups. The new generation's learning is often public, not private, and can be negative, which leads to depression, anxiety, and social isolation. This suggests that we need to learn new ways to develop our social skills in the virtual world.

Participants in our interviews also said that they often experience the impact of an uneven distribution of power and an erosion of ethical behavior within their organizations and on the world stage. Balancing the expectations of the individual and the collective, as well as the broader stakeholder groups within the larger global context, is more challenging today than in the past. Participants thus suggested that a new model must help define new governance models and clarify roles and relationships that are more equitable, fluid, and interdependent. Their feedback also suggested a growing need to learn how Use-of-Self can help create alignment and build effective working relationships even within complex political partnerships and stakeholder groups. This new challenge requires active visible leadership, cross-collaboration, and teamwork.

6. *Teamwork and collaboration extend beyond the internal organization to include external partners and other stakeholders.*

The TIC model focused on teamwork and helping leaders apply participative, collaborative processes to build multidisciplinary teams and to work across the organization. This emphasis is still relevant in the new LMC model, but it needed to extend to working in networks both within and outside of our organizations, such as with partners and other stakeholders.

7. *The work/life wholeness of Use-of-Self is a new focus.*

The previous model of Use-of-Self was about performance at work. For some leaders and highly driven organizations, there was no work/life balance. But today's employees are focused on health and wellness and do not want to burn the candle at both ends. A new need to focus on the whole person is critical in leading meaningful change. Aligning personal purpose with one's role and the organization's purpose is essential. This includes prioritizing and balancing life, work, health, time, and resources when developing Use-of-Self strategies to lead meaningful change.

→ Introducing Use-of-Self 2.0

The new model of Use-of-Self in the LMC Framework thus builds on these themes and the feedback from participants in this research. The new model depicts a process of continuous movement and incorporates the current world context and emerging trends, such as the importance of ethics and building trust in organizations, the impact and influences of technology, sociocultural and economic changes, geopolitical influences, social justice issues, our global and local concepts of community, and our desire for a sustainable planet. The Use-of-Self foundation and principles are now also aligned with the current research on emotional intelligence, neuroscience, and mindfulness.

Figure 4 depicts a new visual representation of the LMC Framework and Use-of-Self that replaces the former TIC diagram you saw in Figure 1. As you can see, this model considers the Use-of-Self in a variety of contexts—individual, team, team of teams, organization, community, society, and planet. It combines them into a dynamic, flowing wave in the form of an infinity symbol, suggesting the never-ending challenges of change, the constant Use-of-Self, and the multiplier effect that can happen on all levels.

Figure 4 The New LMC Framework and Use-of-Self

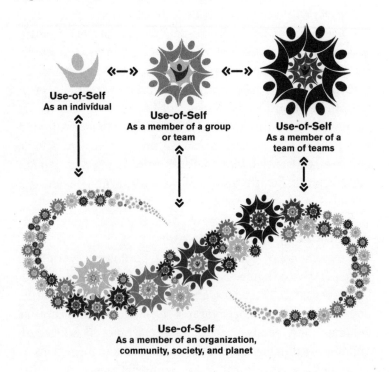

Use-of-Self
As an individual

Use-of-Self
As a member of a group
or team

Use-of-Self
As a member of a
team of teams

Use-of-Self
As a member of an organization,
community, society, and planet

Chapter 2

Six Keys to Guide Your Use-of-Self in the Leading Meaningful Change Process

Developing Use-of-Self is a lifelong learning process. There is no magic formula or one best way to do it. Each individual needs to find their own way. The following six keys have proven to be effective in helping leaders, managers, and change agents to build on their strengths and unlock their old beliefs and patterns that were counterproductive or that blocked them from achieving their desired impact. You could also incorporate these keys in your leadership development plan. The six keys are:

1. Being aware of and accountable for our choices
2. Cultivating Use-of-Self as an instrument of change
3. Reframing
4. Navigating the dynamics of power
5. Giving and receiving feedback
6. Appreciating and leveraging our diversity

Let's explore the six keys to guide your Use-of-Self as you lead, manage, and participate in the LMC Process. For each key, I provide an overview, an example, and an exercise that you can do on your own or with others. In part 2 of the book, you will find more exercises to assist you in working on these keys.

→ **Key #1: Being Aware of and Accountable for Our Choices**

We often assume that we are always choosing to be our best adult self, that we mature with age and make the best choices. However, we know this isn't true. In all probability, at various times in your life, you have behaved poorly, blamed or praised others when they didn't deserve it, or acted out your feelings inappropriately. Basically, you were not living your best adult self.

In our book *Triple Impact Coaching: Use-of-Self in the Coaching Process*, Edie Seashore and I described the link between the choices we make as individuals and the resulting impact that we can have on others. When we are conscious and intentional about the choices we make, we can have a positive impact that starts with ourselves and then cascades to our team, to the rest of the organization, and to the communities that we work with and serve. On the other hand, when we are not conscious and intentional, our choices can have a negative impact on ourselves or others.

So what influences our choices? The Choice Awareness Matrix developed by Edie Seashore and shown in Table 3 highlights the choices we make and how we may attribute them to ourselves or others.

Table 3 **Choice Awareness Matrix**

	Choice Attributed to Self	**Choice Attributed to Others**
Aware	ACCOUNTABLE Deliberate Intentional	PRAISE or BLAME
Unaware	AUTOMATIC Robotic Habitual	SOCIALIZATION Inheritance Adapt Assimilate

Aware of Our Choices

When we are aware of our choices, we are accountable, deliberate, and intentional. We take ownership of our behavior and actions. If we make a mistake, we acknowledge that we made it and take responsibility for it. But if we are aware and attribute our choice to others, we may choose to blame or praise them. For example, you may have worked really hard on something, but instead of acknowledging your own work, you may choose to praise other people like your teacher, colleagues, and even your team. Or if you worked hard on a project and it failed, you might blame someone else for the failure.

This also applies to your use of social media. It begins with your intention and how you want to show up in your communications and the message you want to send. We have seen people use social media intentionally to praise and help others, but we have also seen how social media can be used to harm others. This is one example of how your Use-of-Self, or its lack, can quickly result in a positive or negative impact that cascades from you to the team, organization, community, and planet.

Unaware of Our Choices

Sometimes we make choices even though we are unaware of doing so. When this happens, we are operating on automatic. For instance, think of how you use your phone. When it rings, beeps, or alerts you to an email or a text, do you look at it right away? Do you answer it automatically regardless of who you are with or what you are doing? Even though you may not think you are making a choice, answering the phone is a clear decision.

Many choices we make are based on how we were socialized in our values, beliefs, and culture. For example, in the workplace, you may have been socialized to avoid conflict or respect authority and people in positions of power. If this is the case, you may choose not to challenge your boss or boss's boss when you are in meetings. You may even wait until you are called upon to speak even if you have a valuable contribution to make. Or you may have been socialized to be "in control" at all times and tend to take over meetings and be the most vocal, preventing others from contributing.

Think about what you have assimilated in your life that you choose to focus on in your interactions with people in positions of power and authority. Can you recognize when assimilation (unconscious bias) might be taking over? What choices are you making based on your family culture, professional discipline, assumptions you have about your position and role, and/or any socialization that influences how you show up in your leadership role?

Here is an example of when I resisted change and the choices I made during the installation of a new accounting system to use in my practice. My husband, Don, is my IT guy. He takes care of all our technology and enjoys doing this work. I, on the other hand, am less intuitive and not comfortable with technology. Just as I was leaving to go on a business trip, Don gave me a link to a video demonstration to help orient me to the new system. My first choice (aware: accountable) was that I procrastinated and did not do the prework. When I returned home to do an invoice as I usually do (unaware: automatic), I quickly realized that I had a lot of questions and needed some training. Learning the new accounting system required a lot more time than I had planned. I was worried that I would make a mistake and lose my data (unaware: socialization—I once had a bad experience when I lost my data while working on a project. I also was accustomed to having a print guide or a step-by-step process that I could follow when learning something new). I "chose" to be frustrated and impatient instead of open to new learning. I reacted poorly and blamed Don for not setting me up with a training manual and coaching to make the process easier for me (aware: blame—attributed to others).

In hindsight, my best adult self could have chosen to take responsibility for my poor behavior and for not doing my prework. I was impatient and could have been more appreciative of his diligence in finding a good accounting system and setting it up in time for my return from my business trip. I could have also chosen a better time for the implementation and expressed more clearly what help I needed to learn the system (aware: accountable). This would have made the change process more effective for both of us.

You can use the Choice Awareness Matrix to reflect on how well you are doing in being accountable to yourself and others, and to understand your impact in making conscious and deliberate choices. The matrix helps you reflect on your beliefs, values, perceptions, and behaviors that influence your choices and interactions with others. Awareness of these aspects of yourself enables you to make better choices about how you intentionally want to interact with others and achieve your desired impact.

Choices Made during Change

During any change effort, most people at some point will resist the change. Understanding that resistance and the choices available to each of us helps us be more effective as change agents and in working with others to adopt and support the changes earlier and throughout the process. This has proven to save time, money, and effort, which ultimately leads to the achievement of more effective and efficient business results.

Think of a time when you resisted change. If you are stuck trying to come up with an example, think of a renovation or move that you may have lived through at home or in your office, or when you installed a new technology system or implemented a new business process at work. Here are a few questions about that change effort that can help you reflect on it and explore the notion of having choices as you lead and manage future change:

1. What did your behavior look like?
2. Why were you resisting?
3. What choices did you make?
4. What did resisting do for you?
5. What did you need to accept or adapt to the changes?
6. What was the impact of your choices on others?

Using your example, go back and review the Choice Awareness Matrix in Table 3. Were you aware of the choices you made when you were resisting change? What would you do differently next time?

In my interviews with leaders, I have asked many about their own choices. Here is one executive leader's reflection:

> When I am at my best, I remember that it is not all about me. I slow things down and try to walk in the shoes of others, to deepen my understanding and to gain empathy for what the other person is experiencing. I listen to understand. My internal dialogue goes something like this: "I always have a choice. I make the decision about my reaction and response. I can choose to be reactive or constructive in my Use-of-Self." I no longer say to myself, "You made me...," or "I had or have no choice."

Your beliefs, values, and perceptions influence the choices you make in your thoughts and behaviors, and these then impact your interactions with others and your performance in all that you do. Awareness of self enables us to make better choices and be more purposeful about our intentions. When we are aware, we are accountable, deliberate, and intentional in how we choose to be present, show up, think, and act.

→ Key #2: Cultivating Use-of-Self as an Instrument of Change

Our Use-of-Self is our most valuable instrument in the change process, and the only one that we can control. As a leader, a manager, a follower, an intervenor, a change agent, or any other role that you play, you may be juggling and managing your own reactions to change, and depending on how effective you are, you may have a positive or negative impact on others and, ultimately, on the system.

In their book *Dangerous Opportunity: Making Change Work*, Chris Musselwhite and Randell Jones describe four stages of transition: acknowledging, reacting, investigating, and implementing, as summarized in Table 4.[8] These reflect the typical reactions that people experience when going through a transition process. Musselwhite and Jones state that trying to skip over the stages can lead to a false sense of accomplishment and derail the change. Reacting and investigating represent the most challenging stages of any change process. They are phases when perspectives shift from the old to the new and when most emotional energy is expended.

Given this framework for how people react and adapt to change, the value of Use-of-Self is evident. It is important to pay attention to what you and others need as you go through the change process. What stage are you and others in?

Here is how one team leader described Use-of-Self as he managed his day-to-day operations:

> I am constantly juggling what is needed to lead my team, deal with staff issues and crises, manage the day-to-day operations and develop the big picture, vision, and strategy for my organization. My Use-of-Self is in the midst of it all. It helps me be self-aware by reflecting on my behavior, and the intended and unintended impacts that I am having with my team and the organization. I know that paying attention to my Use-of-Self is instrumental in helping me develop strategies to maintain my resilience, manage my resistance, and be responsible and effective as a leader and manager. It also helps me to help others to do the same. I see the concept as a way of emphasizing the intersection

of my Self with the many other considerations that permeate effective leadership.

As leaders, our goal in leading meaningful change is to understand the dynamics of our own triggers, reactions, and emotions as we ourselves go through the change process so that we can develop strategies to reduce the tension and churn that can occur. When we understand ourselves and are aware of our choices, we are better able to help people in our organizations go through the change and regain their health and productivity as quickly as possible. If we don't lead and manage it well, we can have an exponential negative impact that reverberates across the organization.

Now let's put this concept into practice. Think about a time when you lived through a change. It began with an ending, then there was the transition period, and then a new beginning. You may have experienced this transition process personally when you moved out on your own for the first time, became a parent, or got married, or you may have experienced it professionally when you started a new job or project in your organization. With this change, even if it was expected, you went through a cycle that was something like Musselwhite and Jones's four stages.

With your chosen change in mind, let's examine it in greater detail by understanding more deeply the nature of resistance. The experience of resistance is not the same for everyone. In fact, I suggest there are four distinctive types of resistance: cognitive, political, psychological, and ideological. Being able to distinguish among these four will help you master your Use-of-Self as you experience the phases yourself and as you coach others through a change.

Cognitive resistance is usually the easiest type of resistance to notice. This shows up when people ask analytical questions about change like: What is the logic or rationale for this change? How much will it cost? What are the wise

Table 4 Stages of Transition: Typical Reactions Summary

Stage 1: Acknowledging	People are shocked and feel threatened. They may deny that a change has happened and may appear slower in their thinking, distracted, and forgetful. Productivity may be low.
Stage 2: Reacting	People express a range of reactions: anger, depression, withdrawal, etc. They may try to bargain and keep old ways, and not move or adopt the changes. People may hold out and think that they can "wait and see" if this too shall pass. People may cycle back to stage 1, when their emotions are denied or ignored.
Stage 3: Investigating	People may express grief and sadness but may also begin to explore the possibility of future options. Their willingness to explore new options may be mixed with some reservation. Emotions can range from excitement to anxiety.
Stage 4: Implementing	People appear ready to establish new routines, adapt to new systems, and help others learn new ways. They may be comfortable with the change, be more flexible and creative, and take more risks. The change is viewed not as a "change," but "the way we do things around here."

practices or benchmarks that are informing the change? What is the evidence that we need to change? How do we measure up against our competition?

Political resistance is focused on power dynamics. Political resistance often takes place when decisions are made top-down, or unilaterally, without a real or perceived opportunity for input from others. People may not fully understand the reason for the changes and may react by lobbying or protesting as a group against the changes, refusing to do the work, or conducting workarounds to avoid implementing new policies and procedures. On a personal level, if someone perceives that they may lose their personal power and influence, they may sabotage the changes by not meeting deadlines, blocking the changes, failing to communicate information, speaking negatively about the change, or challenging authority. Individuals may use their personal power and connections with other people and networks in organizations to spread rumors and create confusion, intentionally and unintentionally.

Psychological resistance can surface when people feel vulnerable and perceive the change as a threat to their livelihood, or too big a challenge that will stretch them beyond their capabilities. It can occur when they need to learn something like a new technology or new work processes, but fear that they will not be able to learn at the pace needed or do not have the skills and supports to succeed. Psychological resistance can even show up, surprisingly, in people who have typically been very confident and successful in their role, but who may go through a crisis of confidence as they anticipate the change. They may experience a lack of self-esteem that is demonstrated by being overly critical of themselves, feeling overwhelmed and anxious, and having trouble focusing.

Depending on the type and impact of the change on their personal life and their day-to-day work, people may need help through training and development, coaching, mentoring, and peer support to overcome psychological resistance. In one organization, we implemented peer coaching for two weeks to help people adapt to a new technology system. We provided guides, a toolkit with pictures of the new processes, and a step-by-step instruction manual that they could read on their own and keep handy when they were using the new system. We also tracked their progress daily with a scorecard so they could gauge how quickly they were adapting to the new system by seeing the reduction of errors.

Ideological resistance is the hardest type of resistance to change. Ideology is based on our beliefs, values, principles, and philosophies. Wars are fought over ideologies. In a business example, when I worked in social services during a recession, the organization I worked with had a reputation for delivering the best social service programs in the country. We were committed and proud to be helping people find sustainable long-term employment in their field of training. This meant that if an engineer was unemployed, we would support them until they found another engineering job or equivalent because we believed they would be able to be self-sufficient for the long term. Then we had a change in government that embraced a different ideology, one that focused on short-term assistance and cost reduction. The new philosophy was "any job is a good job." Initially we resisted and questioned the principles and values that were driving the program cuts and the related changes in policy and practices that would make it more difficult for clients to find long-term sustainable employment.

Now that you understand the four types of resistance, you can work on recognizing them in yourself and others. For example, go back to your example of resistance and ask yourself, "What type of resistance was I experiencing at that time? What did I need to move forward?" Or pick a situation when you worked with people who were resisting. What type of resistance were they demonstrating and what did they need to adapt to the changes? The more you understand your resistance, the better you will be at coaching yourself and others throughout the change process.

Technical, Political, and Symbolic Skills

For many years, I have been doing the following Inspiring Leaders Exercise with groups, asking them to select a leader whom they admire the most and to explain why. President John F. Kennedy, Queen Elizabeth, Nelson Mandela, the Dalai Lama, Mohandas Gandhi, Malala Yousafzai, Terry Fox, and Mother Teresa are some of the leaders identified.

Once everyone gives me their responses, I ask them what the leaders they have selected have in common. One theme is consistent in the answers I receive: they are all people who led significant transformation—personally and politically— that wasn't easy, yet they had a huge impact in the world. In further discussion, the group also usually recognizes that the leaders they have identified have three key skills in common: technical, political, and symbolic. All three are essential to lead people through significant change.

Technical skills: All these leaders excelled at getting things done. President Kennedy, for example, was admired for having a technical team who had the know-how to send a man to the moon.

Political skills: All these leaders understood their political context and were effective in working with their internal, local, and global political stakeholders. They used their personal power, both formal and informal, to influence others, build coalitions, and drum up support for their causes. Queen Elizabeth is the world's longest-reigning monarch in history. Nelson Mandela sacrificed his freedom for human rights and later became president of South Africa.

Symbolic skills: These leaders were selfless and worked for a higher purpose. They stood up for their values and beliefs in challenging times. They endured difficult circumstances and personal sacrifice. Their leadership actions and stories inspired nations and generations around the world. Their legacies are symbols for peace, equality, and human rights, as demonstrated by the convictions of the Dalai Lama, Gandhi, Malala Yousafzai, Terry Fox, and Mother Teresa.

Are you using technical, political, and symbolic skills in your approach to leading and managing change? The more aware you become about how you use these three skills in your approach to leadership, the more dynamic you will be in leading change.

→ Key #3: Reframing

Reframing is related to the French word *recentrer*, meaning to be recentered. When you reframe a situation, you alter the meaning you attach to the experience so that you can "see" things in a different way or with a new perspective. Reframing is a powerful process when you are off-center, are doing something misaligned with your values or principles, or need to view a problem, situation, or conflict from a different perspective or angle that you may not have initially agreed with, including how you look at the impossible and make it possible. Reframing can be used to create better choices and strategies to reduce conflict within ourselves or in our relationships. Reframing is especially important in leading change.

Here is a personal example of how I once had to remind myself to reframe an incident. I am not a very good golfer, but I do enjoy the game. Every once in a while, I have a great shot or get par and feel great. I have confidence and want to come back and play again. However, not every shot is a winner. Sometimes I whack the ball too hard, or my ball goes off in the wrong direction and lands in the sand trap or in the rough. When this happens, I often choose to be angry, frustrated, and very critical of myself. I say things like, "Bev, keep your head down. Focus. You didn't follow through. Bev, don't whack the ball. It weighs only 1.6 ounces!" When I keep up this negative thinking and behavior, I can go into a cycle of frustration and disappointment with myself and have a terrible game.

If I choose to reframe my frustration as an opportunity to learn and practice, I am more relaxed, and I do better and enjoy my game. My self-talk usually goes something like, "Bev, good try. That shot was a good miss. Now you can practice your sand wedge! It's not so bad, at least you are getting in your exercise and can enjoy the beautiful view! What could you do differently next time?" The reframing of my errors does not take away the fact that I had a bad shot, but it helps me take a pause, reflect, and think more constructively about my last move. I can choose a different approach for my next shot. I can break the pattern of carrying over my negative thinking and feelings about my performance and my last error and choose to be more positive and constructive. I can also choose to change my attitude and enjoy the rest of my game.

Here is an example of reframing that occurred during a merger that I was consulting on.

I was working with the transition team responsible for leading the second attempt at a merger of two construction associations. We were putting together the objectives for a board meeting that was to bring together the board of directors from both associations, and I proposed that the meeting be designed to reset the plan for the merger. The electricians in the room informed me that the word "reset" in the electrical trade is not a positive thing (it means the root problem was not addressed and it needs more work), so they feared that people would see the first attempt as a failure. We quickly reframed the word "reset" to "continue" to develop our plan. This reframe created more energy and motivation to embark on the second phase of the merger.

In another example, I was working with a team who was getting ready to implement a new organizational structure. They were worried about how people would receive the new structure, since they had already gone through several restructuring exercises in previous years and were promised that there would be no further changes. They were going to use the word "realignment" to explain their plan to implement the new and revised organizational structure. After we discussed the possible unintended consequences of using "realignment," they changed it to "alignment," which was more in tune with the principles behind the change. They wanted to convey the message that change is an ongoing process, so alignment also needs to be an active and iterative process. In this context, the organizational structure needed to be adaptive and responsive to whatever emerges throughout the change journey.

Here is how the reframing process works. The Reframing Exercise involves three steps, which I will explain with examples:

1. Values
2. Psychological opposites
3. Reframes

Before we begin, make a table with three columns, as shown in Table 5.

Table 5 **Reframing Exercise**

Characteristics about Myself That I Value	Psychological Opposites	Reframes

Step 1: Values

Identify two or three values or characteristics that describe you at your best. What does your behavior look like when you are living your values? How do other people experience you when you are living your values? How do you feel when others are living the same values or characteristics that you identified?

Characteristics about Myself That I Value	Psychological Opposites	Reframes
Productive		

For example: I value being productive. When I am productive, I am energized and busy. I have a sense of accomplishment when my work is done and done well. I like working with others who also value being productive because, together, we get things done.

Step 2: Psychological Opposites

Now identify two or three words that reflect the opposite of your values. I call these the "uglies." We all have them. This is when we are not living our values or are not our best self. It is our psychological opposites that reflect our "shadow self"—a part of our behavior that we don't usually like about ourselves. Since we find these behaviors unacceptable in ourselves, we have difficulty accepting them in others. These behaviors prompt us to get into conflict, dismiss others, and even dislike ourselves and others.

Our behavior when we are acting in our psychological opposites can block our ability to see different perspectives or opportunities. It may even block our ability to build relationships and work effectively with others or to be open to new opportunities. Often people don't like to talk about their psychological opposites because they may feel vulnerable and don't want to admit that they act this way.

Some people try to influence or soften the description of their psychological opposites when working with others. However, it is important to be honest about your psychological opposites because it will help you dig deeper to identify your personal values and beliefs that you hold dear. When we are behaving in our psychological opposites, we are usually in an uncomfortable place that is unique to each of us, so the words you select as the opposites of your values should have a true personal meaning to you. The words you choose may not mean the same to someone else.

Identify your psychological opposites. What are you thinking, feeling, and doing when you are not living the values or characteristics that you identified in step 1? How do you work with others who demonstrate the same psychological opposites?

Characteristics about Myself That I Value	Psychological Opposites	Reframes
Productive	Lazy	

My psychological opposite of productive is lazy. When I am lazy, I procrastinate and ignore the important things that I should be working on. I take more time to do simple tasks, and my work is usually sloppy, not up to my own or other people's expectations. I don't feel a sense of urgency or accomplishment. When I work with others who I think are lazy, I am frustrated and don't want to depend on them, so I end up doing the work myself. This is not productive for me or others, which leads to our next step: reframes.

Step 3: Reframes

The third step is to reframe your psychological opposites into frames that help you take a new perspective or change your thinking and actions so that you can be more effective when acting in your psychological opposites. The reframes should be adjectives or adverbs that would allow these behaviors to be acceptable to you. That makes it easier to work with others who demonstrate that behavior. To develop the reframes, you need to reflect on how you feel when you act in your psychological opposites, which may be similar to how others feel when they act in ways that you find unacceptable. Having a reframe ready when you find yourself in a conflict situation may eliminate some emotion from the situation and help you be more constructive in your Use-of-Self and working with others.

Characteristics about Myself That I Value	Psychological Opposites	Reframes
Productive	Lazy	Pacing

My reframe for being lazy is pacing. When I slow down the pace of my work, I feel relaxed and in control. I am more likely to take a break that will help me reenergize and focus. It reminds me to breathe and notice that not everything is urgent or needs to be ramped up to full steam ahead. Also, when I reframe when others are being lazy and choose to think instead that they too are pacing their work, it helps me approach them differently. I can appreciate that they too need a break. This reframe helps me take a different perspective and move more quickly to develop effective solutions that will help us be more productive and that works for them and myself!

Now it's your turn. What are your reframes for your psychological opposites?

→ Key #4: Navigating the Dynamics of Power

The greater awareness you developed in mastering Use-of-Self does not suggest you can make conflict over power disappear. Let's face it: most of us have a love-hate relationship with power, yet it is inherent in all our interactions. We can choose to own our power or give it away. We can choose to empower others or take power away from them. We can also choose to share our power with others or control it. Being aware of how we use our power helps us be more effective at leading, managing, influencing, and empowering ourselves and others.

Sometimes we are deliberate about how we use our power; at other times, we may not be fully aware of our impact. We may need to get feedback from others to close the gap. Regardless of how we obtain it or give it away, we are always making choices about how we use our power—for example, to help ourselves, to help others, or to influence a situation.

How you use power requires understanding four types: personal, formal, informal, and collective power.

Personal power is your unique Use-of-Self that people admire and want to emulate. For example, people may respect your personal charm, your charisma, or a quality in you, such as your ability to communicate. They may admire your expertise, skills, knowledge, and achievements. Others may respect your power because they want to be influenced, taught, coached, or mentored by you. People may follow you on social media to glean your wisdom. People with personal power are credible, trustworthy, good communicators, and able to influence others.

Formal power derives from formal roles, authorities, and accountabilities. Formal power structures, processes, accountabilities, and responsibilities are usually documented. They are spelled out in governance documents, organizational designs and structures, job descriptions, project charters, and contracts. However, even if these formal power structures are written down, formal power is often not enough. We often need to pay attention to and use informal power sources that are less visible.

Informal power is focused on our relationships with people outside of our formal roles and structures. These informal power sources include people whom you may have previously worked with in other parts of the organization, former committee or workgroup members, clients, partners, colleagues, friends from work, and those you may interact with in your community or professional networks, associations, or social clubs.

Collective power is the fourth power source and it comes from belonging to groups with whom you share the same values, interests, or objectives. These may be communities of practice, professional or political networks and workgroups, strategic alliances or partnerships, unions, trade associations, community groups, and any other relevant connections. These groups collaborate and share power.

They often make decisions based on democratic principles and consensus. They speak as one voice for the collective. They also have power in numbers and can influence
as a collective or community. Alternatively, they can be
stakeholder or interest groups that lobby for the interests
of the collective to make a decision or influence a policy or
approach to the change. Depending on their power as a collective or community, they can support and positively influence your change, or disrupt and derail it.

One source of information on power is the book *Napoleonic Leadership: A Study in Power*, by Stephanie Jones and
Jonathan Gosling. The authors studied Napoleon's rise and
fall and drew some lessons for today's leaders that resonate
with the Use-of-Self concept relative to how to gain and
use power on the battlefield, in domestic and international
politics, or in leading complex change in the workplace.
As they point out, the strengths of Napoleonic leadership
can include brilliance in a chosen field, charisma, fearless-
ness, adventurousness, confidence, energy, determination,
passion, vision, and excellent planning and organization
skills. But these strengths also have a shadow side, such as
needing constant acclaim, demanding adulation, callously
wasting resources, assuming constant success, focusing on
self-preserving behaviors, and being egotistical and narcissistic, overly controlling and autocratic, manipulative,
obsessive, and naïve. Jones and Gosling also document how
some leaders like Napoleon resort to questionable strategies to legitimize their power. These include patronage,
meritocracy, charisma, opportunism, manipulation, coer-
cion, popularity, and succession.[9]

Here is an example from my consulting practice of how
all four types of power were used in a change effort. The
project was at a university, and one element of it involved
becoming a more student-focused institution, which would
require everyone working together as a community. We conducted a formal process that included meetings and focus

groups with each of the service area management teams, front-line service providers, support staff, parents, and students to understand what was working well versus what needed to be addressed to improve and enhance student life and the learning experience. We also held a contest whereby the students were invited to make suggestions and identify opportunities to improve and enhance services offered to them. This contest tapped into their collective power and produced recommendations that were well received and represented the voice of the student community. The results were then presented to the formal system for discussions and approvals of the student union, senior leadership team, and other representatives, and were then prioritized and incorporated in the larger strategy.

The senior leaders also "experienced a day in the life of a student," in which they observed a service area other than their own and received services in real time as if they were a student. They also talked informally with people in the community to learn about their ideas to enhance student life and the learning experience. These two activities helped them tap into their informal power and provided unstructured opportunities to connect and learn informally and naturally, which they would not normally do in their day-to-day.

Following these activities, the senior leaders then came together to talk about what they observed and learned through both our formal and informal research processes. The leaders' personal power, or Use-of-Self, played a key role in their effectiveness as individual leaders and as an entire team throughout the consultation process. They put a lot of thought into how they wanted to show up, using their formal, informal, and collective power. They balanced their use of power, being accountable, directive, participative, and collaborative. They were intentional in how they chose to communicate, frame the study, ask questions, and challenge their own and each other's thinking. They were also committed to suspending judgment and being open to new learning. Their individual and collective Use-of-Self had a direct impact on their ability to build confidence in themselves as leaders and as the leadership team. This resulted in trust and confidence in the final plan and the changes that were about to occur. For some of the leaders, this approach was a leadership development opportunity that they embraced. For others, it required coaching, skill development, and learning more about themselves so that they could communicate more effectively as leaders who wanted and needed to influence others to change their behaviors and act differently.

As a change leader, you may find yourself working with all four types of power, or you may find yourself needing to develop your power to be effective in a particular area. We are often not aware of how subtly we may have lost our power, or how unwittingly we give it away. For example, I once attended a presentation given by a young manager to her team, who constantly interrupted her with questions and sideline issues. Her focus on the issue she came to speak about kept veering off into different directions. She gave away her power by choosing not to bring the team back to the key objective of her presentation. She ended up not receiving the approval she needed to advance her project. Not asserting her needs ultimately had a negative impact on her work. People walked away thinking she did not have control of the meeting and that her topic was not important.

Another way to lose our personal power is when we ourselves give it up to someone else. For example, when we hear that our ideas are being credited to someone else and we do nothing to correct this misattribution, we are giving up our power. However, we can just as easily take away someone's power by stepping in and doing their work when they need to do it for themselves to keep their power.

Consider these questions about your use of power:

1. What type of power do you need to be effective in your role?
2. How do you use your power to help yourself?
3. When have you lost your power? What happened and what could you choose to do differently next time?
4. How do you empower or disempower others?

In part 2, you will find the Power Map Exercise to help you map the formal and informal power dynamics that are at play in your work and gain insight into how to develop your Use-of-Self to navigate the situation.

→ Key #5: Giving and Receiving Feedback

Learning how to give and receive feedback is an essential element in developing your Use-of-Self so you can have meaningful conversations with individuals in teams and groups throughout the organization during the LMC Process. Feedback can be a positive and sometimes challenging experience during which we learn about ourselves and the impact of our behavior on others. It can be affirming and validate what we already know about ourselves, but it can also help us learn more about our impact on others, where we are not as effective, and where we may be struggling. Feedback thus helps us grow and develop in ways that we may not have considered before.

People often make some of the following assumptions about giving and receiving feedback:

- I look forward to giving people feedback because only I can help them.
- I need to give people feedback so they can change their behavior.
- I can't give someone feedback because they will be angry with me.
- My feedback will hurt someone because they won't want to hear it.

- There's no point in giving feedback because nothing will change, so why bother?
- I may hear something I don't want to hear. People will see my weaknesses and hold it against me.
- Giving feedback is a career-limiting move.

It is no wonder that people are conflicted and struggle with giving and receiving feedback. Reframing feedback as an educational tool or learning opportunity can make the experience more positive, constructive, and impactful rather than negative for both the giver and receiver.

Here are some questions to help you reflect on your beliefs and assumptions about how you give and receive feedback:

1. When are you successful giving feedback? Why?
2. When are you successful receiving feedback? Why?
3. What makes it difficult or hinders your ability to give and receive feedback?
4. Is your belief system different if you give feedback to or receive feedback from a person in authority or your peers, subordinates, or family members?

A Twist on the Relationship between the Giver and Receiver of Feedback

Feedback is a conversation that takes place between the giver and receiver. It is like an email exchange for which you have three choices: accept, save, or delete.

You can accept the feedback if you believe the message has meaning and matches your perception and experience. Or you can just save it, neither accepting nor rejecting it, because it does not completely match up with your expectations. It may catch you off guard and generate emotions that block your ability to hear the message. Or sometimes you can become so excited or upset that you are not fully present and do not hear the whole message.

In this case, you may save the feedback until you have digested it more fully or for when you have time to follow up with the giver to clarify what they meant, to dig deeper, and to ask questions. Lastly, you can delete the feedback, disregarding it because it does not match your experience. But if you hear the same feedback consistently from multiple sources, you should probably take a closer look at it. It is important to understand that underlying all three options is the fact that the receiver always has control over how they are going to receive and interpret the message.

In addition, consider that feedback always reveals something more about the giver than the receiver. For example, in giving feedback, the giver chooses what is important to focus on. The feedback reflects the expression or interpretation of the giver's own beliefs, assumptions, values, perceptions, and intentions. The problem is, we often fail to remember that the giver is not an unbiased source and is actually a player in whether the feedback process is successful or not. Thus, it is important to look more closely at your Use-of-Self when you give and receive feedback.

Let's look in detail at how a successful feedback process works. When giving feedback, it is important to be aware that you are telling the receiver something about yourself, not just giving the other person a message. In fact, if you think about any time you have received feedback yourself, you can see that the message is as much about the "what" as it is about the "how." People communicate using a tone of voice, emotion, and body language, and from their own lens that reflects what they value and believe is important and meaningful to them. The feedback represents what they desire for your continued behavior or changes that they would like you to make. Given this, to have successful feedback, the giver needs to be cognizant of what they are revealing. The more you disclose about your values, beliefs, and perceptions, the better the receiver will understand your intentions.

On the other side, the more the receiver discloses what they would like to have feedback on, the higher the probability that the feedback will be more meaningful and helpful. As the receiver, it is thus important to ask the giver for what you are seeking from the feedback so that you can increase the chances of getting the feedback you need.

Finally, recognize that successful feedback is a loop. When you are the giver of feedback, you don't know how effective you've been in communicating your message unless you check back with the person to see how the message was received. The receiver interprets it based on their experience and perspective, which the giver may not know. Then, when the receiver responds or reacts, the giver may also have a reaction to the receiver's reaction.

The complexity of this process may explain why the message, after going through all the filters, may not have the effect that the giver intended in the first place. This is why, in order for the feedback process to be truly complete and successful, the giver needs to follow up with the receiver to learn how the message was received and, if necessary, further refine the message to make sure it was heard as intended. The giver thus actually has the responsibility in this final phase to verify that the feedback was received in the way it was intended.

I call this final phase the "flexion point." It is precisely the point when the right choices can make feedback successful and valuable. The giver and receiver need to take this extra step to listen more deeply to each other and learn about each other. The giver can learn how the receiver thinks and whether the way the feedback was given helps the receiver accept and use it. At the same time, the receiver can learn how the giver thinks and what they value.

Here are two suggestions to help improve the feedback process:

1. Be clear about what the feedback is about. Why does the giver want to give it? What does the receiver want to receive feedback on? How will the feedback help both people? The answers to these questions will help clarify expectations for both parties.

2. Share expectations at the beginning of any meeting in which feedback is being exchanged, such as a team meeting or a coaching and mentoring session. This can be very powerful in helping individuals and teams establish guidelines, principles, and norms for giving and receiving feedback. This same process can be applied in large group settings to help you engage and collaborate with your employees and stakeholders.

Feedback Structures

You can create formal and informal opportunities to exchange feedback.

Formal feedback is probably the one we are most familiar with and use most often. This takes place through such structures as performance reviews with a manager, at project milestones when reviewing lessons learned, or in debriefing sessions. It is usually planned and scheduled, and it may be influenced by other agendas that are not totally controlled by the receiver of the feedback. For instance, your organization may do performance reviews or client surveys at a scheduled time that is coordinated across the organization. You don't always have influence over when these events will be administered, but you do have choices on how you will respond to the results.

Informal feedback is, in my opinion, the most effective way to give and get feedback. It can be exchanged at any time. Both giver and receiver can have more control in the shaping of the feedback. The informal exchanges allow for multiple rounds of discussion between the parties to clarify the information and learn about each other. I often give or take

informal feedback when having lunch or dinner with colleagues or clients. The informal setting can prompt more
honest and transparent feedback. It can also lead to more
unsolicited feedback, so remember, if you are the receiver,
you always have control in how you accept and interpret the
feedback.

Anonymous feedback offers mixed results. Some people appreciate that it provides an outlet to say things they
may not have the courage to say face-to-face to someone or
in open conversation. But some use it to vent, to dump, and
even at times to harm people. As a result, it may have less
impact than the two methods above. It loses its relevance
without a proper frame or grounding in context, objectives,
and timing.

Anonymous feedback can be effective in the right circumstances. For instance, it can be useful to get a quick
pulse or reading on what is happening, such as a reaction
to a presentation. Be careful though, as we may give or
receive anonymous feedback believing it is useful when in
fact it may not be meaningful or change anything if there
is no relevant context and follow-up. An example of useful
anonymous feedback I witnessed was when a senior leader
administered an online survey after every employee forum
to obtain feedback on the senior management team's ability to create a shared vision for change. He invited employees to provide their input about the change plan and how
the team could ensure the forums met employee needs. People could sign their names if they wanted to do so, but most
did not. The management team looked at the comments and
presented a new action plan back to the participants. In general, it proved to be a successful method to obtain feedback.

A lot of organizations administer anonymous employee
engagement surveys. These may provide some useful data,
but leaders and managers need to follow up and dig deeper
to truly understand the meaning of the results.

Practice Feedback Sessions

Practice sessions are a good way to improve your feedback process in challenging situations. For example, if you are seeking feedback on your project, you might practice with a trusted colleague or colleagues, having them watch you in action and critiquing it honestly. This can offer a more natural way to obtain feedback close to the moment when you need it most.

I often work with teams to help them prepare for presentations on their change plans. One of our exercises is to develop an elevator or hallway speech about the change. They are given two minutes to practice and then do a roleplay. In coaching them, I ask them a few questions so I can have a lens for understanding what they are seeking for feedback. I ask questions such as the following: What is your intention or objective for this presentation? What do you need to know about the receivers or stakeholder group that you should anticipate or pay attention to (e.g., their level of resistance or their lack of knowledge on the issue)? How do you want your message to be received? What about your Use-of-Self do you want feedback on?

I often hear the following responses to such questions: "I want the audience to be inspired and agree to be part of the change, because right now they are resisting. They don't fully understand how the changes can be positive for them. For feedback on my Use-of-Self, I want you to let me know if I am talking clearly about my message and if my tone was engaging and inspiring. I would also like to know if you could relate to the examples that I used. Finally, I would like to know if I inspired you to take action and be part of the change."

As you can see, this type of practice Q & A session can help people clarify their needs for feedback.

In another example, I once worked with a colleague who asked me to give him feedback on his listening skills. He was aware he dominated discussions in meetings, seldom providing room for others to participate with their ideas and inputs. He did more talking and less listening. Given this, he asked me to give him feedback whenever I saw him overtalking and not listening so that he could become more self-aware of his behavior. He wanted to learn what he was thinking and feeling in the moment so that he could learn to catch himself sooner and adapt his behavior for the benefit of the whole team. We worked together for several weeks, during which I provided feedback to him after each meeting. Little by little, he found that he began listening more and getting better collaboration from the team.

Another example is when I conducted an exercise with a leader who was working in his second language and wanted feedback on how well he communicated. The first time he made a presentation, it was clear that he was very awkward, cumbersome, and self-conscious. I asked him to do the same presentation in his native language, and he excelled. This practice helped him realize he could succeed in his first language, which gave him more confidence. He drew from this experience and developed new strategies that helped him speak more naturally with audiences in his second language.

Observing Your Use-of-Self as Feedback

Rather than wait for others to give you feedback, you can also develop feedback skills by observing yourself and watching the impact of your behavior on others. Keep a journal to track the patterns you find and chart the progress of your behaviors.

For example, one new manager was struggling with getting his work done while simultaneously training his team of new hires. He was often frustrated because they took longer than he expected to get their work done. He found himself working a lot of overtime to catch up on his own work because he was constantly doing everyone else's.

His boss gave him feedback that his approach was not helping the team and that he should develop his coaching skills. He accepted this comment and agreed to work on it, knowing it would be good for himself, the team, and ultimately the organization. He started keeping a spreadsheet of when he did well coaching his team versus when he jumped in to do their work. He monitored the context of each situation, reflecting on what he was thinking and feeling that prompted him to act in the way he did at that moment and writing down what he observed. The exercise helped him become more aware and intentional about his beliefs and choices. From that, he was able to develop a plan to correct his behavior and express what he needed from his team in a timely and effective manner.

In the part 2 toolkit, the Coaching Conversation Exercise will help you practice giving and receiving feedback.

→ Key #6: Appreciating and Leveraging Our Diversity

Truly appreciating your own diversity and that of the people in your organization and external stakeholders is necessary to develop an inclusive, engaged, and highly productive workforce, community, and planet. Every individual is unique, special, and valuable in their own way. There are many types of diversity: age, gender, sexual orientation, family status, education, professional training, social experiences, values, beliefs and traditions, religion, language, geography, country of origin, organization and work cultures, and more. Such wide diversity enhances how we live, work, and play.

Our world and workplaces today are complex environments, which makes it all the more critical to go beyond just appreciating our differences to actually leveraging the uniqueness and diversity of people. The wide range of individuals, teams, and organizations we encounter allow us to learn and benefit from our differences so that we can work in harmony across boundaries in our workplaces, communities, and societies.

Here is what one senior leader had to say about his Use-of-Self when working with emerging leaders in his organization who were different from him. I find his statement a beautiful expression of the openness to diversity and the desire to learn from others that can help a leader grow.

Use-of-Self requires empathy and the capacity of both understanding your impact and your ability to put yourself in the other person's shoes. I am an older person working with young people entering the workforce. I believe I understand their dreams and challenges because I too did an MBA and have worked and traveled internationally. But this is so far from the truth. I need to slow down my impulse to jump in and listen more carefully for connections and shared experiences. I realize people are going through similar experiences, but I may not always pay attention to their personal experience in the same way. I sometimes assume I know them, when in fact I don't.

I need to consciously work at being aware of my own biases and pay attention to their unique experiences, backgrounds, and values that influence their work and life. Not all students are the same. To be effective, I need an open mind and to stop filtering my interactions and conversations based on my own values, beliefs, or experiences. I need to validate what's really happening. What am I really hearing and experiencing? I need to notice. Listen to learn, learn to listen and understand. I need to do this in my work and at home. My Use-of-Self requires me to be humble and receptive to developing a solution, the way forward, or a point of view that is different from my own.

When I listen to myself speaking, I need to remind myself that my point of view may be inappropriate. It may not be relevant today. I may need to be more open and adapt to listen for understanding. If we don't do this as the boomer generation, we may turn off younger generations. Today's youth need to find things out for themselves.

It's not all about me. I need to walk in their shoes. I am reminded that Use-of-Self is a continuous process that requires the attention of my whole being.

Here are a few questions to help you and your team identify, appreciate, and leverage your diversity. If you ask these questions in a group setting with your team, you may be surprised to find out much more about each other than you ever expected.

1. Where were you born and brought up? Where were your ancestors from? How does your background influence your life today?

2. What was your family life like growing up? What is it like now? What values and traditions do you live out today that you learned from your family? Are there some you don't honor? If so, why? How is your family life different or the same today as when you grew up?

3. When did you first realize that you were unique, different, or special in a significant way? What was the impact on you then and now?

4. What significant events have you experienced that have shaped your life?

5. What unique contribution do you bring to your work, life, and/or community that you would like to leverage as you work with others?

→ Mastering Your Use-of-Self

The quest for mastering Use-of-Self is a lifelong journey and is worthwhile working on regardless of your age, gender, stage of life, or career. Your Use-of-Self is the one thing that you can control in the midst of any change occurring in your life. All six of the keys reviewed in this chapter will help you become more self-aware, intentional, and accountable for your thoughts and actions. Mastering them will also help you learn about, manage, coach, and mentor others as you lead meaningful change. Going forward, your Use-of-Self will help you be more present so that you can live your best self and make a positive difference in all that you do.

Chapter 3

The Leading Meaningful
Change Framework

In this chapter you will be introduced to the LMC Framework. I want to begin with a personal story about my background in this field, which led me to derive many of the principles of the framework and to my belief in the value of leading change using the process that I will explain.

As a reminder, the Use-of-Self plays a critical part throughout the entire LMC Framework. As the prior chapter emphasized, it is at the core of and necessary to creating and leading meaningful change. As you review and understand the LMC Framework in this chapter, keep in mind that your Use-of-Self is constantly at play in implementing these principles.

→ My Story: Learning about *Meaningful* Change

I began my training in a program called Special Care Counselling at Vanier College in Montreal in 1978. It was a fairly new program at that time, designed to educate individuals to work with special needs and vulnerable people. Between this three-year program and my subsequent job as a childcare worker, I learned the fundamentals of systems thinking, group dynamics, program design and evaluation, facilitation, and coaching. In addition to classroom instruction, we were supervised at our client sites, in real time, as we completed three field placements. We also participated in peer learning groups where we reflected on what we were doing in our placements and obtained input and feedback from each other that helped us advance our learning. This was the beginning of a lifelong learning and doing process that I continue to practice 40 years later.

This journey has taught me that to be effective in helping people learn and adapt to change, leaders have to consider the person with whom they are working as part of a larger system. This means developing empathy for them as human beings, walking in their shoes, and considering their day-to-day and the systems they interact with or that influence them in order to co-develop with them an approach and plans that will motivate and empower them to achieve the desired goals and objectives. The individuals and groups of people with whom we work have to be motivated and feel as if they are truly part of the process to develop, implement, and evaluate the plan. The activities, tools, and techniques of change must be customized to meet their needs and enhance their work. It is also important to understand that when you make a change in one part of the system, it can have an impact on other parts that will also need to be considered in order to have sustainable change.

My first deep experience with this precept was in 1996 when I was working full time at the Regional Municipality of Ottawa–Carleton (now known as the City of Ottawa) in the Social Services Department. At that time, I was the supervisor of a team of welfare workers and a member of the district area management team.

In the previous year (1995), a new provincial government had been elected on a conservative platform focused on reducing the size of government, lowering income taxes, and creating more jobs. With this platform, the government launched a significant reform in the delivery of social services, including a reduction in welfare benefits and the number of people on social assistance. As part of the makeover, the Ontario government embarked on a "business transformation project" that was a technological overhaul of the province's welfare system. A number of fraud-control mechanisms were put in place, including the creation of a single province-wide welfare database, expanded information sharing among government bodies, and an automated eligibility review process.

This was a radical change from the way we worked under the previous government. Prior to 1995, we provided the highest rates for financial assistance for those in need across the country, but we also had the highest number of people receiving assistance as a result of the 1990–91 recession. The philosophy of our social services programs was rooted in supporting unemployed people to be self-sufficient not only in the short term, but for the long term through education, job-search assistance, and training programs until they secured long-term sustainable work. But the new government was less patient and declared that social assistance was meant to be temporary, so any job was a good job.

These top-down changes were sudden and not well received. I remember the day the cuts to social services were announced over the radio. We had no prior knowledge of what they would be. We, the management team, met in the boardroom and listened to the radio announcement while our staff were doing the same at their desks. Our clients received the same information via radio as we did, with no follow-up plan to address their needs or concerns.

Many of us, myself included, were conflicted, as we were not aligned with the values and principles that guided the new policies. This was a philosophical shift for us, one requiring a significant transformation in our culture, not only for those of us who were leaders, but also for our teams, clients, organization, and community. I realized I had to dig in and figure out what our people needed so I could lead and manage through these upcoming changes. As a management team, we had to be thoughtful in our approach to the change, so at that time, it felt like we were building the plane as we were trying to fly it.

As a public servant and supervisor, I was responsible for honoring the democratic process that elected the new government. I had to lead my team to implement these changes, even though they required us to dismantle many of the very programs and services that we had built in prior years and that we believed were having a positive impact on our clients and the community. I knew that I personally had to work on my Use-of-Self to be effective as a leader, given the context of our new world and my own personal uncertainty and resistance to the way the changes were being led and managed.

Over the next days, the management team met with our people to talk about the impacts of the changes. The savings targets were set, but there was no plan for how to achieve them. It was our first experience of leading organizational change in this manner as a municipal government, and for me as a leader of change. Within our department we had the skills to coach our clients through the personal journey of job change, but we were unprepared to do this for ourselves.

For the entire year that followed, we lived with uncertainty, not knowing who was going to have a job and who would be let go, myself included. This situation created a lot of fear, anxiety, confusion, and discontent. People were also concerned and skeptical about the approach to change. Many believed it was driven solely by the financial targets, technology, and templates. We received information only on an as-needed basis, so we did not fully understand the purpose, overall plan, or process. It was a perfect storm of how not to do change.

With the support of my colleagues and as part of my graduate studies (in the Master of Applied Social Science program, now called Applied Human Sciences) at Concordia University while working full time, I designed a survey that went out to all staff across the department to assess what was needed to lead and manage this change. It was the first such survey ever done. Its questions were designed to explore how people were thinking and feeling about the changes and what they needed in terms of skills, knowledge, and abilities to lead, manage, and implement the new directives.

From the survey results, we learned that 76 percent of the respondents did not have previous training in organizational change, so we created a leadership development program for the staff, including all supervisors, managers, directors, senior managers, and the commissioner of social services, to help us learn new ways to work together and develop the skills to lead and manage change in our department.

The experience of developing and delivering this program was life-changing for all of us. Our commissioner played an active role in engaging people at all levels, seeking their input, and leveraging the expertise of the business transformation team who were developing and overseeing the change strategy at the corporate level. He was a great role model, communicator, and advocate for our clients. He addressed issues, squashed rumors, and kept his finger on the pulse of people's reactions to the changes throughout the process.

We simultaneously developed people at all levels of the organization. We sought to put everyone on the same page and helped them understand the need for change. People rallied together around a common purpose and understood how they could be involved in the process. All training materials were customized so they could be applied to people's real work—and vice versa, with our real work challenges and examples being used to inform the learnings and adapt the change plan as needed.

Through this experience, I learned that meaningful change cannot be achieved simply by driving a tactical or transactional plan to implement new processes or technologies. It has to have meaning by making sense to the people involved and those impacted by the changes. People want and need to be involved, developed, and empowered. I also learned that the change process needs to be grounded in a shared purpose and supported with a coordinated plan that is integrated and aligned with the strategic priorities of the entire organization to address the business needs. It needs to attend to and, as necessary, shift the organizational culture—all at the same time.

→ The Guiding Principles of the LMC Framework

This experience was a catalyst for change in my personal and professional life and propelled me into a career that I never would have previously imagined. It is for these reasons that I began the journey of developing people to lead meaningful change. The lessons I learned then, and from the clients and colleagues with whom I've worked over the past three decades, remain relevant today. These experiences led me to develop the following seven guiding principles that can be applied to any change project, regardless of size and complexity. These are the principles of the LMC Framework today:

1. Create a shared purpose, vision, principles, and values.
2. Develop and engage people.
3. Build relationships and foster teamwork and collaboration.
4. Develop the plan to align with strategic priorities and goals.
5. Develop a unified organizational culture to support change.
6. Set up systems, structures, and processes to support the change.
7. Conduct a continuous evaluation of the plan, actions, and impacts.

These principles are critical, with each one building on the next to create a holistic change environment that has meaning for everyone. Let's take a look at each of them.

→ 1. Create a Shared Purpose, Vision, Principles, and Values

The *process* to develop a change plan is just as important, if not more crucial, than the change plan itself. Creating a shared purpose, vision, principles, and values that people understand and agree with allows them to see themselves as active participants in the change journey rather than as passive followers. A shared purpose captures early involvement and support for the change, reduces tensions and conflict, and leads to better results. A shared vision and surrounding principles and values behind it act like a compass that guides individuals, teams, and the entire organization throughout the change journey.

In his book *The Purpose Effect: Building Meaning in Yourself, Your Role, and Your Organization*, Dan Pontefract describes the importance of understanding the interconnection between personal, organizational, and role purposes. He states that when all three purposes are aligned and congruent, it delivers a balanced state that he calls the "sweet spot" because it results in a multiplier effect that brings out the best performance in leaders, employees, teams, customers or clients, and, most importantly, society as a whole.[10] In other words, when all three purposes are aligned and enacted, everyone wins.

Creating a shared purpose is not an amorphous exercise. There are numerous strategies you can implement to co-develop the purpose, inviting everyone to participate in the process. Your ongoing and conscious Use-of-Self is especially valuable as you use such strategies to

- gather and share information with others to create a common understanding of why the change is needed;

- ground the change in research, wise practices, and evidence and then share it;

- envision and share what success looks like as you or your team, department, or organization lead others through the change;

- be out there among the people—walking around, observing, and talking with them in their workplaces and communities about their challenges and hopes for the future, and sharing what you are learning and planning;

- observe and listen to customers, clients, partners, and stakeholders;

- facilitate discussions and working sessions to bring people from different areas of the organization together to learn about the context for change and make collective sense of the information and potential impacts;

- seek input and feedback about the results of the interviews and consultations to inform your decisions and be open to possible adjustments to the change plan and process; and

- frame and communicate the change honestly and authentically about how you are going to lead, manage, and involve people in the change process.

In chapter 6, you will read about the Envisioning Success Exercise, which you can adapt to create your shared purpose, vision, and guiding principles to help you lead meaningful change. In chapter 7, we will explore the strategies that the senior leadership team at the City of Ottawa used to create a shared purpose that was embraced across the corporation.

→ 2. Develop and Engage People

Organizations today comprise multiple generations working together in their workplace. In our fast-paced environment, organizations need to develop people in real time. They must put in place succession plans, coaching, and mentoring as well as on-the-job training to develop and engage people throughout the process. Learning and development are therefore critical.

In my experiences, I prefer a blended learning approach that uses both formal and informal learning. In both cases, the learning is also customized so that we can "use work, not make work." In other words, the goal is to provide people with opportunities to ground their learning in their real work as they learn, practice, and apply new concepts and skills in real time. This approach ensures that the learning being done in a formal classroom setting or working sessions, and/or informally through social interactions, can be applied and sustained between sessions and thus have a real impact in their workplace.

Informal learning has become increasingly prevalent in many workplace environments. Human resources professionals and operational leaders believe that employees themselves may be initiating informal learning to a greater extent than previously thought. The Conference Board of Canada's August 2018 report *Informal Learning: A Spotlight on Hidden Learning in the Canadian Workplace* cited the Workplace Environmental Index (WEI), which measures 32 rated elements representing both the quality and state of an organization's work environment and the strength of its learning culture. The study showed informal learning has increased to 62 percent and formal learning decreased to 38 percent among the participants in the survey. More revealing is that 78 percent of the respondents spend up to two hours per week on self-directed learning on the job.[11]

Employers need to be clear about the role of workers when it comes to their learning and development, versus the role the employer should play. The data suggest that employees are okay with a level of shared responsibility when it comes to their learning. Nevertheless, research shows that senior management support for learning and development is essential. This includes explicitly supporting and approving resources needed for informal learning. Organizations should invest in informal learning activities that are likely to have the greatest payoff, such as coaching and mentoring. In Canada, strong WEI organizations are four times more likely to offer coaching to their employees compared with moderate or weak WEI organizations. Employer-supported conference attendance and mentoring programs are also important. Results indicate that strong WEI organizations were three times more likely to offer both of these learning opportunities to their employees than moderate or weak WEI organizations.

In 2016, the Conference Board produced another report, *Employee Engagement: Leveraging the Science to Inspire Great Performance*, based on data from a survey of 400 Canadian employees and a ten-year longitudinal database of engagement surveys that established the Conference Board of Canada's employee engagement model.[12] This research showed that while organizations understand the importance of having an engaged workforce, it is not clear what exactly engagement consists of and how it can be used to improve organizational culture and performance. However, the model highlights key workplace characteristics that drive employee engagement. These are grouped into seven distinct factors or drivers that have been proven to be associated with highly engaged employees:

1. *Confidence in senior leadership:* Organizational goals are communicated to employees and there is a strong sense of trust that senior leaders can attain those goals.
2. *Relationship with one's manager:* Managers value their employees' opinions, provide constructive feedback, and follow through with their commitments.
3. *Interesting and challenging work:* Employees believe their work is varied, interesting, challenging, and meaningful.
4. *Personal and professional growth:* Employees believe there is a clear career path with opportunities to grow within their organization.

5. *Acknowledgment and recognition:* Employees believe their work contributions and accomplishments are recognized and not taken for granted.
6. *Relationship with co-workers:* Employees' co-workers share information willingly and work together as a team.
7. *Autonomy:* Employees have a say in their goals and objectives and how the work gets done.

This research, along with my own experiences in developing programs to support people leading change, shows the need for learning and development in real time throughout any change process. People want to make a difference. They are in search of meaning in their work and they want to develop the skills necessary to do it. They want to be involved in the process. Therefore, how we engage and involve others need to be thoughtful and relevant and result in actions that help people develop the mindsets, values, behaviors, and skills they need to be successful.

→ 3. Build Relationships and Foster Teamwork and Collaboration

Change initiatives are often complex, involving multiple stakeholders from inside and outside the organization and at various organizational levels. Given the fast pace, high impact, and complexity of change, it is essential that you build relationships with trust, confidence, and empathy among those you lead, work with, and serve, as well as among those who may be impacted in the change process. In this regard, you need to develop two key levels of outreach.

The first is an effort to create strong interpersonal relationships. Your ability to meaningfully connect and build trust and credibility with another human being is critical. You need to be empathetic—able to walk in the shoes of the people you lead, manage, and serve. This starts with finding ways to fully understand and appreciate their situation and context. Investigate their wishes, worries, needs, and concerns. When people know you are empathetic, they will feel heard, appreciated, and understood. Being able to relate to others and appreciate their views will help you become more effective in making the change meaningful to them. In my view, effectively building interpersonal relationships is what makes the work of leading change worthwhile, enriching people's lives one by one.

Also keep in mind that to improve interpersonal relationships, leaders need to not only find ways to keep a finger on the pulse of how people are reacting to the change, but also actively seek to understand how their reactions impact ours. Such a two-way effort helps produce more meaningful conversations and a deeper, shared understanding about the change. Here again, awareness of your Use-of-Self plays an important role. We learn from each other how to create tighter alignment with the shared purpose, to leverage skills and knowledge, and to identify the talents of other people so we can design and implement solutions that produce results that are far greater than what one individual could have achieved on their own.

The second level of outreach is to develop teamwork and everyone's ability to collaborate with others across and beyond the organization. Teamwork can take many forms, as people may work in a variety of groups: functional, departmental, service, multiprofessional, multidisciplinary, virtual-mobile, global, teams of teams, cross-departmental teams, and project teams, to name but a few. Individuals may also be a member of teams outside the organization, such as in the community or in a charitable organization. People may also be stakeholders, partners, consultants, advisors, or coaches working with others inside the organization. Lastly, someone may be the client or recipient of services or a user of the product. Regardless of the type of team one is on, or whether it is internal or external, collaboration is an essential skill for success in any change effort.

What does good collaboration look like? Here's how I describe it. You have good collaboration when you create cohesive teams that are able to get along with each other and collectively work to achieve the desired results, not driven by egos or personal self-interests. They are continuously learning and adapting to circumstances as the change occurs. They are committed to a shared purpose. They trust and respect each other and feel a strong sense of belonging. They are accountable to each other and the organization. They can count on each other when times are tough and are effective working together to develop strategies, solve problems, and make decisions. They can be more efficient and act in less time, spend less money, and achieve better results when they collaborate and work with others. Cohesive teams create a positive and fulfilling workplace culture. They are dedicated to developing others. At their best, they are role models and set the tone for the organizational culture that promotes cross-company teamwork and builds partnerships inside the organization and with the community.

Henry Mintzberg, in his book *Rebalancing Society* and in the CoachingOurselves topic of the same name (see chapter 6), talks about the need to rebalance society.[13] He says that we need to challenge destructive practices and create constructive ones in the organizations where we work, the communities where we live, and the governments we elect. A healthy society balances the collective power of governments in the public sector with the commercial interests of businesses in the private sector and the communal concerns of the citizens in the plural sector, which are our communities, charities, not-for-profits, clubs, etc. Rebalancing begins with the grounded engagement of ourselves, each of us and all of us in our communities, as citizens, and as consumers. Thus, we and organizations in all sectors need to function at our best, which means as communities of human beings, not collections of human resources.

In chapters 5 and 6, we will explore further the dynamics of teamwork and how to build and develop teams that are able to lead, manage, and influence others to embrace change and participate meaningfully in the process.

→ 4. Develop the Plan to Align with Strategic Priorities and Goals

A successful change plan requires careful thought, expertise, and alignment with the overall organization's strategies and goals. A plan that is at odds with the larger organization's priorities and that lacks the appropriate supports is doomed to fail.

A 2015 global survey conducted by McKinsey & Company revealed that the most effective transformation initiatives involved four key actions: (1) role modeling, (2) fostering understanding and conviction, (3) reinforcing changes through formal mechanisms, and (4) developing talent and skills.[14] No single action was more important than the other. All four actions were critical to shifting mindsets and behaviors. The more actions that were used, the more likely executives were to rate the transformation as a success.

But the most intriguing response to the survey was that transformations were more likely to succeed when leaders took a systematic approach to obtain input from a wide range of stakeholders and then prioritize the resulting initiatives according to the organization's strategic goals. When all of these elements fell into place, 76 percent of transformations were successful, compared with 22 percent when none of these elements were present.

The LMC Process that you will read about in the next chapter uses what I call the Master Change Plan approach designed to align the strategic priorities, project plans, and supports with the organization's larger purpose. This systematic approach is critical to avoiding numerous common problems that organizations often encounter in a change effort, such as these:

- The change lacks focus, or it is too narrow.

- The change effort needs political support, but the leaders don't know how to influence the decision makers.
- Projects stall or are at risk because they lack funding, resources, or people.
- The plan is overwhelming because of too many competing priorities or not enough time or people to meet the commitments.
- The change is confusing or feels disconnected because people don't understand the bigger picture.

→ 5. Develop a Unified Organizational Culture to Support Change

Leading meaningful change requires a deep, shared understanding of the organization's culture. You develop this by collectively experiencing and studying the culture to understand how it evolved, why it exists, and what elements need to change or be sustained over time for success. Changing organizational culture is complex and must be analyzed at each level of the organization, inside and out.

In his CoachingOurselves module *Probing into Culture*, Edgar Schein, a noted thought leader in organizational development, defines culture as follows: "Whenever a group shares a common experience, a culture emerges." He describes corporate culture as "the deeper level of basic assumptions and beliefs that are shared by members of an organization, that operate unconsciously, and define in a basic take-it-for granted fashion an organization's view of itself and its environment."[15] In his book *The Corporate Culture Survival Guide*, Schein describes three levels that we need to examine to understand organizational culture:[16]

- *Artifacts:* The visible organizational structures and processes in an organization
- *Espoused values:* Implied in the strategies, goals, and philosophies that guide the behavior of the people in the organization

- *Underlying assumptions:* The unconscious, taken-for-granted beliefs, perceptions, thoughts, and feelings that influence day-to-day actions

All three levels combine to create the explicit and implicit organizational culture that leaders and staff viscerally feel each day, no matter what might be stated otherwise.

Here is an example of how a senior leader, Pierre, who worked in a travel business, was surprised to learn about his organization's culture through the eyes of a group of new employees. As the vice president, operations, Pierre had hired this group and soon learned they were unhappy and were considering leaving the company. He was shocked and wanted to find out what had gone wrong. Listening to their complaints, he learned they were frustrated because they felt the new ideas and innovations they offered were often shot down. The decision-making process was too slow for them, and there was a lot of red tape. Ultimately, they believed they did not fit into the company's culture.

Attempting to rectify the problem, Pierre held a meeting to explore a strategy that could close the gap between this group of new hires and the long-term service managers. Both the old and new groups of employees were asked to come to the meeting with an artifact, a story, or an experience that spoke to how they experienced the organization's culture. One new employee who was recruited for his expertise in the service industry was tasked with revamping the interior design of the product line, and he brought a bedspread to the meeting. He commented that this same design for the bedspread was used in the organization for over ten years and was out of date. He used data from customer satisfaction surveys to validate his comments and proved that younger customers agreed it was outdated.

Prior to this meeting, the new employee had approached his manager and asked to change the bedspread so it would be more modern. His idea was shot down. He was told that he couldn't order a different bedspread because the item could only be ordered from the current supplier, who did not carry new designs. "That's the way things are done here," he was told. Of course, the new hire was deflated and felt this small innovation would be an easy one to accept. The manager who had rejected the idea was at the meeting and, up to this point, had not realized the impact of his decision.

The discussions during the rest of this meeting created a shared experience that helped both groups better understand their culture. In the end, they agreed to challenge the way decisions were made and evaluate when old assumptions were outdated and possibly worth letting go. In this way, they learned about their organizational culture and what was important to hold onto versus what could be let go.

In another case, I was having trouble understanding the background information that a new client sent to me because the documents were full of unexplained abbreviations. When I asked the company for a lexicon or dictionary so I could understand the abbreviations, they emailed me another 100-page document! After I caught my breath, I slowed down and reflected on this type of organizational culture. I concluded that the lexicon was more than an explanation of terms. It actually represented an honest attempt to create a common business language that would be used across the company, regardless of employee rank, gender, race, or nationality. In this way, it validated the challenges of being a global company following a series of mergers and acquisitions. The company represented over 27 countries, with employees speaking multiple languages and reflecting multiple professional disciplines, each of which also had their own business terms and national and regional languages. It turned out that the company was having difficulty implementing a change effort and needed to find ways to orient people to a new organizational culture.

As you can see, language plays a key role in shaping culture, especially when introducing change. It can be difficult to keep up with the pace of new words and special phrases developed to accompany the change if you are not part of the group who created the language. Developing a lexicon, briefing notes, or a list of frequently asked questions can help get everyone on the same page. On the other hand, using abbreviations is not for every culture. One organization that I worked with stopped using abbreviations completely because they were getting in the way of communicating clearly and simply.

The Secret to Shifting Culture

In my work with managers from the City of Ottawa, we learned that the special magic of successful culture change lies in perceiving it not as a single large transformation, but rather as a series of small shifts occurring over time among many groups of stakeholders. This approach helped us become more purposeful about each shift and articulate more clearly the organization's need for the overall cumulative change.[17]

In an article I wrote a few years ago for Queen's University, I described culture shifts as follows: "Culture shifts are smart adjustments in organizations that are created through a series of changes that result in different ways of working and being in relationship to each other."[18] Culture shifts are often initiated through the implementation of new business models, organizational designs, business processes, technologies, or all of the above. Often, these changes are complex, with both planned and unexpected impacts that make them challenging to lead, manage, evaluate, and sustain over time.

As you implement change in your organization, examples of the culture shifts you may experience include moving away from a hierarchical culture to a flatter organization with fewer spans of control and more accountability and decision making at lower levels of the organization; shifting your leadership values to focus more on collaboration and staff engagement and less on a command-and-control style of leadership; or redesigning your organization so that it is more customer-, product-, or service-oriented, which requires shifts in the way people work together. Regardless of the type of change you are implementing, mastering the principles and practices of culture change will impact the way you design, lead, manage, and sustain meaningful change.

→ 6. Set Up Systems, Structures, and Processes to Support the Change

Organizational Systems

To fully understand and successfully implement the change we seek to make, and why it is important, we need to take a systemic view of the entire organization.

Consider how the people involved in any change effort are actually a system in themselves. We are all connected and influenced by each other in how we live, work, and play, especially today through the use of technology and social media. Organizations are human systems that are constantly emerging and evolving as a result of each individual's interactions with their internal and external environments. As an individual working in an organization, we may be a member of many human systems—our team, department, service area, product group, various committees, and so on. Externally, we may be a member of a professional network or a board member of an association, community group, or social club. Lastly, we may be a member of a family, which itself has its own systems. In addition to these human systems, we interact with technological systems that support our business processes and communications.

As you can see, these are all systems and networks in which we interact daily, so we need to consider a wide array of people when we lead meaningful change. We interact with many systems that may be interdependent, so making a change in one part of the system may impact many parts. In leading meaningful change, we need to understand the interrelationships of the people, culture, external and internal environments, and community involved to fully understand the impact of the changes that we want to make.

Here's an example of failing to think in terms of human systems in favor of what appeared to be a simple tactical solution to a problem. The director of an organization wanted to reduce the expense of the organization's real estate. He provided employees with state-of-the-art computers so they could work from home more often, and he rented a smaller office for when people needed to meet in person or with a client. One group did not agree with the change, so the director conducted an experiment that he thought would prove the positive impact of his change. He gave up his office for one month and used his phone and laptop to work in the "new world of the mobile office."

He soon discovered that his experiment created confusion and frustration because people did not know where he was and found it hard to reach him when they needed his advice or approval. As well, the space he had leased was too small for the growing demand for the group's services—their work was often political and sensitive, requiring room to talk and collaborate privately as a team, and they needed an office to meet clients.

In another example, an organization I consulted with had centralized the photocopy and printing machines in one area of its large office. The idea was that the organization would save money by purchasing fewer but larger machines that were cheap and fast. On paper, the plan sounded good, but the leaders of the change forgot to consult with the people who used the machines day in and day out. These people complained that the machines were placed too far from their offices and that the time it took to go to the distant machines was distracting and contributed to increased downtime and errors, which negatively impacted their clients' experiences. To prove their point, they logged how many steps they walked to get their documents for one week. Surprisingly, they were walking approximately four and a half miles (seven kilometers) per day just to go to the printers! As a result, the company altered course and created additional photocopy and print stations in strategic locations across its offices.

Taking a systems approach requires a relationship mindset. The changes you are leading are part of a system with many moving parts. To ensure you are conscious of your intended impact and to be adaptable and responsive to any unintended consequences, you need to ask questions like:

- What does this change do for each individual?
- Knowing what we know now, what is the impact of the change on the team or other parts of our organization?
- Are any mismatches emerging between our intentions and the desired impact?
- What is the impact of the change on our service or product? Our clients?
- Who else needs to be included in our work?
- What may be influencing the change from the inside and outside of our organization?
- What are the risks that we need to consider? What will happen if we don't attend to the risks in the short term? In the long term?
- Do we need to revise our change plan?

When we change one part of the system, it can change another part and possibly create an unforeseen ripple effect in other areas. Looking at and analyzing change as part of a larger system shines a light on unintended impacts and possible risks that may need to be managed. You need to remain open to issues you hadn't thought of, as well as new ideas and possibilities that come forward. You need to remain agile with your change plans and willing to incorporate diverse perspectives and innovative solutions. In essence, the change effort must remain flexible as new issues or ideas develop.

Organizational Structures

Organizational structures are also required to facilitate and sustain change. Depending on the nature of the change, the structures can be temporary, transitional, or long-term. They may be captured in formal organizational charts or maps that make explicit the relationships between people and the interdependencies in governance, accountabilities, decision making, influence, business processes, work flows, and the development and delivery of products and/ or services.

For large-scale change, it can be useful to plan for small and impactful changes in the system that will culminate in a series of culture shifts that, over time, achieve the transformation. Such large-scale changes include implementing a new organizational structure and alignment process, restructuring jobs, redefining the roles of the various levels of the organization, increasing collaboration through employee engagement at higher levels across the organization, building partnerships with other departments and political external stakeholders, implementing new business, product development, and process improvement processes, and executing succession planning and leadership development strategies.

→ 7. Conduct a Continuous Evaluation of the Plan, Actions, and Impacts

It is very important to regularly monitor and evaluate the change journey. As the saying goes, "What gets measured gets done." This requires putting in place a formal process to assess the objectives of the change and how well people are doing as they lead and manage the process. Evaluations help ensure that the change plan is achieving the desired outcomes and impacts. If discrepancies or anomalies are found, you can focus on the best next steps to ensure ongoing adoption of the change, thus increasing the team and organization's performance and achieving faster and better results.

The evaluation process should be meaningful and conducted over time. It should also consider the flow of change, including what is planned and what emerges, as well as the pace and rhythm of the change. Whether the change is developmental, transitional, or transformational, it is important to put in place ways to measure, monitor, evaluate, and sustain it. My sense is that we do not ask often enough—even with a brilliant plan—what we should *stop doing* or modify to reflect the reality of the change as it is taking shape.

Depending on the complexity of the change, you may have multiple projects underway at the same time, each one possibly not at the same stage of change. Each needs to be evaluated separately, and all of the results then need to be compiled into a comprehensive evaluation process. This will help you keep your eyes on the bigger picture and be more purposeful about how you measure, adapt, and coordinate your change plan to ensure you achieve the intended impacts and business results while also being responsive to the unintended ones that may arise.

Conducting a regular evaluation of the plan, its actions, and its impacts helps you ensure the continuity of the positive culture shift and changes that you are making over time, and spot those that are not working. Consistent reviews inform leaders and help them develop a shared understanding of whether people are adopting the changes, demonstrating the new values and behaviors, and achieving the desired results. A comprehensive evaluation process helps leaders work more collaboratively and think strategically and operationally, while at the same time constantly learning and developing themselves in a fast-paced, ever-changing environment.

Evaluation feedback needs to come from multiple sources at all levels of the organization at many key stages during the change journey. This type of evaluation is dynamic, not static. Think of it as taking photos throughout a long vacation and, when it is over, putting them into an album to tell the narrative of your trip. You are capturing moments in time—snapshots of people, activities, and places visited. Sometimes you need to use a panoramic lens, other times a wide-angle, and other times a macro for a close-up shot. Eventually, at various milestones, you put all the photos together so you are able to see themes, patterns, and synergies that give you insights into the change journey so you can understand and appreciate where you came from, where you are now, and where you want to go in the future. This process is also a way to test the pace of your change. Depending on the feedback you receive, you may need to slow down or modify your approach.

In an article I co-authored for Queen's University we describe an approach that measured and evaluated the alignment, integration, actions, and impacts at each stage of a transition process at the City of Vaughan.[19] At one point in the organization's journey, we received feedback from participants in a working session that they did not fully understand the vision, and as a result were not fully aligned. We then slowed down the process and adapted our original plan by adding another working session, coaching, and supports from the design team. This process helped the leadership team to maintain momentum, build capacity, and refocus as they developed and implemented their service excellence strategy.

The LMC Process you will learn about next uses many types of evaluation metrics. You can measure employee engagement through pulse surveys, consultations, and interviews. For other key stakeholders like clients, you can conduct group interviews or site visits. You might engage in conversations during management or staff forums, hold leadership working sessions, or conduct leadership and team assessments. You may also include a review of operational performance and service delivery and other metrics that may be relevant to your particular organizational context.

These seven principles are the compass that guides the LMC Process. Let's take a look now at each of the four stages.

←——————————→

Chapter 4

The Four Stages of the Leading Meaningful Change Process

The field of change management has grown considerably over the past few decades. There are now many models that organizations can use to develop and guide their change journeys. Over the years, I have worked with the ExperienceChange model developed by Greg Warman and James Chisholm of ExperiencePoint. This model has seven steps designed to build a shared vision, commitment, and alignment among key stakeholders and engage others across the organization to support and implement change. The seven steps are:

1. *Understand* the need for change.
2. *Enlist* a core team of stakeholders to work on a solution and scale it.
3. *Envisage* the opportunities and implications of the new solution on the organization.
4. *Motivate* people by connecting at an emotional level around why the change is needed.
5. *Communicate* the vision and mobilize stakeholders around how to roll out the solution.
6. *Act* by taking steps to align the people, structures, and processes with the new solution.

7. *Consolidate* by reinforcing what is working and
exploring what is not working.

The first three steps are designed to align the key stake-holders, while the next four are designed to engage the rest of the organization in the change process. This Experience-Change model is very effective in illustrating the steps to develop and implement a change plan.

However, much like the ExperienceChange model, most change models that my clients have used over the years have focused solely on change management and did not incorporate into their processes the Use-of-Self or concepts of change leadership. Based on my own research and practice, I have therefore developed a different change model, the LMC Process, that includes all three elements—Use-of-Self, change leadership, and change management. All three elements are critical and featured in the LMC Process to help organizations follow a chronology of thinking and acting when undertaking transformation of any size.

In addition, the seven principles of the LMC Framework you just learned about guide a leader's or a team's Use-of-Self in leading, managing, and implementing the change effort. These principles strengthen the four-stage LMC Process that I have created to ensure that the entire model is grounded in the holistic precepts that contribute to making the change *meaningful* to all involved.

Figure 5 illustrates the four key stages in the LMC Process: alignment, integration, action, and renewal. These stages are constantly in play during the design, delivery, and evaluation of people's experiences and the achievement of results throughout the change process. You may use this process for one project, or it can be scaled up or down, depending on the complexity of your work. Let's walk through the stages one by one.

Figure 5 The LMC Process

◄──── Continuous cycles of evaluation to measure results and impacts ────►

→ Stage 1: Alignment

Focus: Planning and developing a shared purpose and alignment with vision, values, and strategic priorities

This first stage is focused on developing the plan to create alignment with the strategy, shared purpose, vision, values, and priorities. It requires the organization's senior leaders and others to research and define the purpose of the change. They then need to ensure and articulate that the change or direction aligns with the organization's overall purpose, vision, and values. Effectively, if a culture shift is to succeed, it must be aligned with the organizational purpose, vision, mission, and strategic priorities. The goal of this stage is to ensure change leaders at all levels understand their role in leading and managing the change journey and that it is in sync with the organization as a whole.

Depending on the complexity of the change project, the process is often best done by forming a design team composed of a cross-section of people who bring diverse thinking, experiences, and approaches into this preliminary planning work. The design team might include representatives with multidisciplinary or cross-functional expertise from the business and support functions such as human resources, organizational development, communications, continuous improvement, and/or process improvement.

Stage 1 Alignment Checklist
Check off the elements you have in place for this stage of alignment.

☐ Engaged champion(s) and leader(s) to actively lead the change

☐ A shared understanding of the need for change

☐ A shared understanding of the plan or the "plan to develop the plan"

☐ Clarity, commitment, and alignment regarding the purpose, vision, and priorities for the change, and the principles, values, and behaviors that will guide it with
  - yourself in your role and as a leader
  - the executive team
  - middle management
  - the front line
  - clients
  - political stakeholders
  - partners
  - other stakeholders
  - the community

☐ An effective governance and organizational design that outlines accountabilities, delegated authorities, and decision-making processes that are defined, understood, and followed

☐ An understanding of the executive/leadership team's role and contribution to the change process

☐ Meaningful participation from all relevant stakeholders:
  - yourself
  - internal stakeholders
  - external stakeholders
  - partners
  - others

☐ Defined language to guide your communications at all levels of the organization and beyond

☐ Teamwork and collaboration where required

They may also be members of the governing board of your organization or people from outside, such as clients, partners, political stakeholders, members of the community, and external consultants. Combined, these people will offer diverse perspectives, insights, and ideas that will enhance your research and analysis and help you understand more fully the organizational culture, its challenges, and what is required for success in this change effort.

In addition to developing the plan and process, the design team's mandate is also to align the program with the organization's mission and strategy, as well as test the feasibility of the program's design, content, delivery, and supports before, during, and after the program. By working together, the design team can facilitate faster and more efficient knowledge transfer and skill development, a shared mindset, and alignment, resulting in a more sustainable culture shift.

Here are questions for the design team or the leader to consider when working through this stage:

1. Why is this change important? What meaning does this change have for you and the people you lead, work with, and serve?
2. Do you believe in the change?
3. How will your employees, clients, and stakeholders benefit from the change?
4. What would motivate them to be involved in the change process?
5. Are you creating alignment on the need for change and developing a shared purpose, vision, and values? How?
6. Do you have alignment with the people you need to help you or who will be impacted by the change? Do you have their commitment to and support for the plan?
7. How does your change align with and support your organization's vision, purpose, and strategic priorities? Are there synergies and/or disconnects?

8. What culture shifts do you need to make to achieve the change?
9. Who needs to be involved to lead and manage your plan? Are they informed, engaged, and participating?
10. Is there any resistance?

The alignment stage should not be taken lightly. Leaders and participants on the design team need to invest in a serious study of the organizational culture to understand how it evolved, what is considered sacred and must be kept, and what is open to change. Consider this stage as a project that can take months, a year, or even longer depending on the complexity of the change. Aligning an executive leadership team and relevant stakeholders to the point where they truly have a clear and shared understanding of the plan, the vision, the direction, and their roles and accountabilities can take more time and effort than you may imagine.

The Alignment Checklist (page 92) is a tool that lists the critical responsibilities at this stage. This worksheet can help ensure your planning is comprehensive and has accounted for the essential tasks that need to be accomplished in this phase.

→ Stage 2: Integration

Focus: Application of learning and development

Leaders are often sent to "training" to learn new concepts and skills associated with the change plan, yet they are not supported to continue their development upon return to their workplace. They struggle to integrate their learning into their work and life. To ensure the sustainability of change, the plan and process must be designed to account for meaningful integration of learning and work, in real time. This usually requires customizing the program content and development process to ensure participants use their real work and life experiences as the basis for reflecting, experimenting, and applying their learning. If this is not done, there is a risk of additional stress and burnout from having to juggle unrealistic expectations, multiple priorities, and additional work.

Learning experiences are most valuable, meaningful, and relevant when they add value to the participant's work and life. The key is to engage people and motivate them to master and integrate the new concepts, skills, and learning back into their real work and to teach, coach, and empower others to do the same.

Here are some questions to help you determine what you need to do to successfully complete the integration stage:

1. How are you integrating the shared purpose, values, principles, and behaviors into your strategy or plan?
2. How are you leading, managing, and communicating your plan to others?
3. What actions can you take to ensure people understand the relationship and impact of the change to their work and life?
4. What processes and structures do you have in place to develop people to lead, manage, and participate in the change process?
5. Do you have a way to measure how well you and others are integrating your learning and changed thinking and behavior in your day-to-day work and life?
6. How can you customize your change approach and tools so they are easy for people to grasp and apply in their work?

Once the change process begins, leaders, staff, and employees may need to adopt a new perspective, behaviors, and skills. However, initially people often resist change and may struggle with applying new learning to their real work and life. Despite retraining, they often revert to their old ways of thinking and doing their jobs. Customizing the content and tools so they have actual meaning and application in people's real jobs is therefore essential. The key is to design the learning so people can use their real work and life experience as the basis for reflecting on, experimenting with, and applying the new skills. Working on real projects has been proven to be more effective than working on hypothetical research or academic case studies. Real projects stem from actual challenges that people are held accountable for and must act upon.

The choice of learning projects should be based on tangible needs that people have in their workplace. The projects should help people reflect on the tasks and decisions that they deal with given their span of control and influence. Through such projects, they can understand the purpose of the change and adapt to it voluntarily and willingly. It's also important that the change projects be linked to the strategic priorities of the organization. This "use work, don't make work" approach helps everyone engage meaningfully in the process and ensures that the work being done in a classroom setting or informal and social training can be applied and sustained between sessions and thus have real impact in the workplace.

To increase the probability of success and sustainability over the long term, I recommend that learning projects (which I also call "change challenges") be assignments people can complete on their own, or as part of a project team, or with leaders who are attending the working sessions. The projects should be within the participants' span of control or authority and supported by their immediate managers. Ideally, the projects should also be aligned with the department's strategic goals and designed to support each individual's personal learning objectives. In this way, people can take pride in what they have learned about the change and the role they play in contributing to it.

Here is how one senior leader in a mining organization developed a learning strategy to establish a culture of safety. This culture shift required changes in both mindset and behaviors of people working in the corporate offices and in the field. The company provided workshops and training for all employees and tracked how well they were doing using regular feedback they received from the teams. They also created a number of performance indicators that they tracked. They then communicated the results at regular team meetings. All meetings opened with "safety moments" that highlighted the new principles and best practices to follow, a story about incidents that occurred or were avoided, and lessons learned. This culture shift was significant for the organization. They were effective at integrating training with real work, which led to sustainable change over time.

Change Leadership Challenge Exercise
Here is a brief look at the Change Leadership Challenge Exercise to help you integrate your development with your work. Completing this exercise at the beginning of your change, midway through, and at the end is a great way to reflect on and evaluate the culture shifts and effectiveness of your leadership and the plan. In the part 2 toolkit, you will find complete instructions for this exercise and an example of how one person completed it.

1. Describe your change project or leadership challenge:
    a. What is the context (factors influencing the change: internal and external forces for and/or against the change)?
    c. Why is it important to address this project or challenge at this time?
    d. What are the objectives, deliverables, and expected outcomes?
    e. Who are the key stakeholders who need to be involved in the change?
    f. How will you measure success?

2. Describe the anticipated impact of the change on the
    a. people
    b. culture

Here is a checklist to help you assess that all the elements for stage 2 are in place.

Stage 2 Integration Checklist
Check off the elements you have in place for this stage of integration.

☐   A baseline to measure how well you and others are doing throughout the change process, including
  - pace of change
  - progress on your plan, deadlines, and commitments
  - successes and challenges
  - skill development
  - adoption of change
  - culture shifts

☐ Customized materials, examples, tools, and processes that help employees understand and integrate the concepts and changes in their work

☐ Customized stories that demonstrate successful changes or movement in the desired direction

☐ Integration of the purpose, principles, and values to guide and communicate the change, including language, materials, and methods

☐ An approach to measure and evaluate the executive and/ or leadership team's development and impact throughout the change process

☐ Self-assessments or formal evaluations conducted before, during, and after the change to understand how the change is integrated and to obtain feedback

☐ Surveys, interviews, and evaluations from individuals and teams that provide input on how they are adopting the changes in mindsets and behavior that demonstrate active and visible change in the desired direction

☐ Integration of the changes in the business

☐ Quick wins and results that are moving in the desired direction

    c. process

    d. technology

    e. structure

3. Provide an overview of your project or initiative:
   a. Where are you in your project plan?
   b. What key milestones and results have you achieved?
   c. What successes have you achieved?
   d. What is helping you to be successful?
   e. What are your challenges or learning opportunities?
   f. Where are you blocked, stalled, or needing some assistance?
   g. What is preventing you from being as successful as you would like to be?
   h. How ready are your key stakeholders to participate and engage in the change process?

4. Describe your learning goals and objectives:
   a. Where are you having the most success leading and managing your change leadership challenge?
   b. Where are you having the most difficulty?
   c. What impact do you want or need to have for success?
   d. What are your goals and objectives?
   e. What key questions or hot topics would you like to address that would be most helpful to you and your team as you develop your change plan or strategy?

→ Stage 3: Action

Focus: A continuous and dynamic cycle of action, learning, and reflection about planned and emergent impacts

The essence of the change effort occurs in stage 3, where the action really begins to take place. The focus of this stage is to participate in a continuous, dynamic, and multifaceted cycle of learning, action, and reflection as you implement the plan and respond to the planned and emergent impacts along the way.

The action phase is not static. It must be done with an awareness that even the change can change. Any actions must remain open to adaptations as new information and feedback come in. The organizational environment is a living laboratory in which the processes of observing, reflecting, planning, acting, and evaluating are iterative, dynamic, and interactive. As soon as we inter-ACT with the system, we can expect a re-ACTION. This dynamic is always at play. At times our action may achieve our intentions, while at other times we may encounter unexpected reactions.

Either way, taking action propels us away from doing nothing to doing something. Even small progress allows us to gain confidence as we learn about ourselves and others, especially the impact the change may have on the larger system. Ultimately, taking action helps us make more informed decisions that lead to deeper and more impactful interventions on all levels.

In this stage, we especially need to notice and become aware of the impact our actions have on others. We can do this by walking in the shoes of others. Seeking to understand their world, we develop empathy and deepen our understanding of the shared values, norms, and cultural implications that are constantly at play when we interact with others. While moving forward with the change plans, a corollary goal is thus to ensure that people are intentional in their Use-of-Self; they need to be aware of the choices they make and the impact their actions have on others. In this way, people learn how to be more effective as leaders, observers, participants, and ultimately intervenors.

The typical change project or initiative usually has a beginning, middle, and end. However, we know that this is not how change happens. In reality, it is complex and can get messy. People go through their own personal experience of the change, layered by whatever else emerges in the process. Individually, as a team, and collectively, we need to pay attention and reflect on the impacts of the planned and emergent changes, and our actions and reactions to them. This rich learning will further inform our choices and actions. In addition to being leaders and implementers in the action phase, we need to be observers and intervenors throughout the process.

Here are some questions to help identify the emerging themes, patterns, and issues that may arise during the action phase. These questions can be asked at key milestones, checkpoints, and/or at the end of a project. You can also adapt these to use with teams.

1. What are some of the most exciting moments that you experienced working on this project or leadership challenge? What happened? Who was involved? What did you do?

2. Why was this experience so special or meaningful for you?

3. How did you live and model the shared purpose, mindset, values, and behaviors?

4. What fears, worries, obstacles, or barriers did you face?

5. What about this experience are you choosing to share with others?

6. What are you keeping to yourself? Why?

7. What personal leadership challenges did you need to overcome in order to be successful?

8. Where in this process did you resist or experience conflict or stress? What did you do? Were your actions effective? What would you continue or do differently?

9. What supports do you need to sustain your leadership development?

And here are some questions to measure and evaluate the success of your efforts in this stage:

1. How are you living the purpose, mindset, values, and behaviors that you want to model as a leader?

2. Are you achieving the results you expected? If so, why? If not, why not?

3. What is emerging that you did not expect and that now needs your attention?

4. What are you learning that you need to continue to do or do differently?

5. What culture shifts are required for success?

6. How effective are you at communicating, engaging, and collaborating with others?

7. What are you doing that is effective in helping others learn and grow?

8. What are your personal and team leadership challenges and development priorities going forward?

Here is a checklist to help you assess the work of the action stage.

Stage 3 Action Checklist
Check off the elements you have in place for this stage of action.

☐ An approach to track themes and patterns from shared experiences, actions, and learning

☐ Measures to assess the culture shifts

☐ Meaningful feedback from meetings and pulse checks

☐ Quality work

☐ Achievement of desired results

☐ Demonstrated successes

☐ Plans to mitigate risks and adjust when there are missteps

☐ Delegated accountabilities and formal and informal power structures that are clearly understood and acted upon at all levels

☐ An understanding of your Use-of-Self and the impact of your actions on what was implemented, changed, or adapted

☐ Individual and/or team development plans

☐ Self-rating and/or formal assessments of the individual or team to assess the desired mindset, competencies, and behaviors

☐ Behavioral measures to assess the adoption of change

☐ Insights, observations, and experiences from personal leadership reflection questions and journals

☐ Frequency and quality of participation in coaching and mentoring discussions

☐ Quantity and quality of work, reflections, and impacts reported in project team meetings and informally between structured learning and working sessions

Measuring the Impact

This stage of the LMC Process is also focused on measuring the impact of the leaders, teams, and collective actions on advancing the change initiative and desired results for the people involved and impacted, as well as for the business, community, and the planet. While I discuss this as a discrete element, as I emphasized earlier, evaluation and measurement are really part of an iterative and fluid process that takes place throughout the entire LMC Process, within each of the prior stages—alignment, integration, and action. It is also part of stage 4: renewal.

→ Stage 4: Renewal

Focus: Evaluation of the overall change and planning for its sustainability

The renewal phase is an important part of the LMC Process. It is designed to conduct an overall evaluation of the change process. This evaluation should be done at critical milestones, at the completion of the project or process, and/or just before you begin the next phase of the work or change plan. Stage 4 focuses on reviewing and evaluating the overall strategy, results, accomplishments, and missteps to determine why and what worked well. What needs to be improved? What about the organizational culture, structures, processes, systems, changes, and insights need to be sustained or regenerated to ensure success in the long term or the next phase?

At this stage I often ask people, "Based on your experience leading this change, what advice would you give to a colleague about to embark on a similar journey?" Almost no one says that you need to pace yourself. This is a long game. Take care of yourself. Take time to reenergize and ensure you have balance. Pay attention to your personal and family well-being. I have seen a lot of people who were very passionate and worked extremely hard to lead meaningful change, yet by the end they were exhausted and had experienced personal illnesses, relationship breakups or divorces, and problems within their families. Those who did well had balance and paid attention to their personal goals and well-being throughout the process. They put in place supports that helped them, such as coaching, mentoring, and regular get-togethers with their peers and colleagues. They also established boundaries between work and family time, participated in regular exercise and fun activities that brought them joy and grounded them, and had healthy eating habits.

If leaders drive change too hard, they may influence an organizational culture that will be out of balance and result in high staff turnover. If this happens, you may need to rethink the pace and sustainability of the changes. Alternatively, you may have been very successful and can take time to renew the team and organization's commitment to itself and the way forward.

Even if you've achieved success, it is important to reflect. Here are a few questions to help you reflect on the impacts of the changes and your actions:

1. How are you evaluating and measuring the impact of your plan?
2. Are you achieving your desired results and impacts?
3. What work is left to do?
4. Do you need to work with other people or be involved in other projects or initiatives to advance your plan and achieve your desired results?
5. What are the risks you need to attend to?
6. What are you learning about yourself, your team, and your organization?
7. What do you need to bring forward and continue in your next steps?
8. What did you learn about the organizational culture that you need to pay attention to as you plan your next steps?

9. Are the changes accepted and incorporated in the day-to-day way of working?
10. How are people affected by the change?
11. What did people learn about themselves?
12. Was the plan too aggressive or too slow? Did it burn people out?
13. Did the organization lose people because they were required to work too hard?
14. What do you need to enhance the team, project, or product?
15. Is the organization ready for the next phase?
16. Do you need to include new people and ideas?

The answers to these questions may reveal that the change effort is actually not fully done and that one or more of the stages in the four-stage LMC Process needs further attention, modification, and/or renewal.

The checklists for stages 1, 2, and 3 are effectively reminders to do an ongoing evaluation. Measuring the impacts at the individual, team, organizational, and community levels throughout your change process provides rich data, deeper insights, and often new strategies that can sustain the changes, leadership development, and culture shifts beyond your project, working sessions, and planned activities.

This checklist (page 107) can help you assess that you have all the elements necessary to evaluate the success of the change effort throughout the four stages of the process.

In part 2, you can complete an exercise called Evaluating and Sustaining Meaningful Change to see how well you are doing in each stage of the LMC Process and develop a plan for your next steps. There is also an exercise called Stakeholder Analysis that will help you evaluate where your stakeholders are in terms of their acceptance of the change plans. This exercise will also help you reflect on the technical, political, and symbolic strategies you need to employ to reduce any stakeholder resistance and respond to their concerns.

Stage 4 Renewal Checklist
Check off the elements you have in place for this stage of renewal.

☐ A process to monitor, measure, benchmark, and report on the plan, results, and impacts achieved (people, business, financial, time, quality, process, service, and product improvements)

☐ Culture shifts that are embedded as a way of working and incorporated in
  - behaviors
  - day-to-day operations
  - service delivery
  - product development
  - policies and procedures
  - checkpoint meetings
  - annual and quarterly reports
  - manager forums
  - training and development activities
  - presentations
  - other aspects of the business

☐ A process to connect all inputs to assess and report on the depth and breadth of the business impacts and adoption of the culture shifts

☐ Reviews, surveys, and pulse checks that demonstrate increased confidence, satisfaction, and positive feedback from
  - senior management
  - leaders
  - managers
  - direct reports
  - operations
  - political and governing stakeholders
  - clients
  - partners
  - others

☐ A process to communicate success stories and lessons learned

☐ Qualitative and quantitative measurements of the impact of the changes on employees' health and well-being, performance, and/ or learning

☐ Strategies, plans, and projects to renew and sustain change, innovate, and go to the next steps

In the City of Ottawa case study in chapter 7, you will read about how the four-stage LMC Process was used to help the city's senior leadership team design and implement a significant transformation affecting all city services by fostering a culture of One City, One Team.

→ Tracking the Change Effort Using a Master Change Plan

Now that we have reviewed the LMC Process, I want to introduce you to a change management tool to help leaders, especially those on the design team, ensure that they can manage the entire process with forethought and accountability. I designed this tool, called the Master Change Plan, to avoid the common pitfalls that I have seen in organizations working on change. I cited a list of them earlier:

- The change lacks focus, or it is too narrow.
- The change effort needs political support, but the leaders don't know how to influence the decision makers.
- Projects stall or are at risk because they lack funding, resources, or people.
- The plan is overwhelming because of too many competing priorities or not enough time or people to meet the commitments.
- The change is confusing or feels disconnected because people don't understand the bigger picture.

The Master Change Plan is a useful template to help you think through, track, and diagnose where you are in the change process. This tool allows you to annotate the entire change effort so that you can plan, integrate, and align the work that occurs during all four stages of the LMC Process. Going through the Master Change Plan process—i.e., filling out the template—is a great way to look for errors and test the feasibility of your plan to see the interdependencies, intersections, and factors that may influence it. Completing the template as a team or a team of teams usually leads to greater efficiencies in the way people work, saves time and money, creates alignment on the way forward, and enhances teamwork and collaboration across the organization and beyond.

Preparation for Filling Out the Master Change Plan

As mentioned, you can use any change model as the foundation for starting this process. For our purposes in this book, I will use the four stages of the LMC Process that incorporate Use-of-Self, change leadership, and change management.

Begin by reflecting on a change leadership challenge you may be facing now or soon. Where do you stand in terms of the LMC Process? Consider these questions:

1. Where are you in the change journey?
2. Why is your change necessary?
3. What needs to change?
4. Who should be involved?
5. How are you going to inspire and empower people to support and adopt the changes?
6. How are you going to develop the change plan?
7. What is your change plan?
8. How will you measure success?

Filling Out the Master Change Plan

Now let's review the Master Change Plan tool that I use to align and integrate a change project with an organization's larger change or transformation. The process includes thinking about and planning for five key areas: the change journey and timeline, corporate alignment, project, supports, and communication. I will start at the top of the chart in Figure 6 to explain each area.

Timeline and Change Journey Rows

Each column in the chart represents a period of time. Depending on your project, you might use the business cycle of quarters (Q1, Q2, Q3, Q4) or a monthly timeline. This chart

Figure 6 **LMC Master Change Plan**

Q_ Where do you expect to be in the change process?	Q_ Where do you expect to be in the change process?	Q_ Where do you expect to be in the change process?	Q_ Where do you expect to be in the change process?
CORPORATE Identify the corporate milestones, activities, and interdependencies that will influence your project and change plan. Monthly/Quarterly Report • Quarterly Production Forecast • Quarterly Cost Forecast • Board Meeting			
PROJECT Identify the key milestones, activities, and interdependencies that will be addressed in your project plan.			
SUPPORTS What structures, processes, leadership development, networks, and supports will people need to build the competencies to lead/manage this change/project?			
COMMUNICATIONS What key milestones, processes, and supports do people need to effectively communicate, understand, and engage with your plan?			

is set up to reflect four quarters, so if you use months, you need to expand the chart to 12 columns.

Using the timeline you decide on, write down in each column of the second row an answer to the question, "Where do you expect to be in the change process?" To answer the question, use the four-stage LMC Process. For example, are you creating alignment, planning for integration, taking action to implement and/or evaluate change, or renewing it? As mentioned, you could also use the seven steps of the ExperienceChange model or any other change model to map your time frame with the steps of that process.

Your answers will help you see how your work aligns with your organization's larger purpose and anticipate where you think people might be in each period. This is a preliminary assessment of your plan; as you implement it, you may need to adapt it based on feedback you get and what you observe, experience, and hear from others.

Note that some of you may be working on large-scale transformation with multiple projects happening at the same time, or you may be in different stages of the change process, so you may need to break down the steps of your plan into individual Master Change Plans that you will eventually roll up into a single Master Change Plan. Others may be working on a single project, so filling out the template may be easier. Whatever your situation, keep in mind that change is a dance between the work that needs to be done and the people involved in the process. This is not a linear process; depending on the complexity of your change, your dance may differ from others.

Corporate and Project Rows
Next, in the corporate row, identify the corporate or institutional activities and milestones for each period, such as checkpoint meetings and presentations to governing bodies or committees for input, decisions, or approvals. It's useful to note key corporate activities or interdependencies that

you need to consider if they might influence your project and change plans, such as reports, budget processes, production forecasts, or board meetings.

After that, use the project row to map the key activities and milestones that will be addressed in your project plan.

It is useful to think about these two rows together as you flesh out your answers. Most people tend to start thinking only about their project without regard to the corporate milestones and activities, but this can lead to a misalignment between the project and the larger organizational strategy. This part of the exercise may reveal opportunities to adapt the pace and sequencing of the project, build capacity, or deal with political issues that may arise.

An example of this comes from my experience working with a learning and development team of six people who were responsible for the leadership development strategy for their organization. When they mapped out their project based on what they envisioned as the ideal sequence, they realized they had 60 activities to deliver in the first two quarters of the year, but nothing mapped out for the balance of the year. They were also a team of just six people with a finite budget. At first they were overwhelmed and believed they could not pull off this plan. They needed to collaborate with people from other departments and access more funding to deliver the plan.

Taking a step back, they used the Master Change Plan process to realign their learning and development strategy to the larger human resource and communications strategies and their organization's vision and strategic plan. This helped them identify opportunities where they could partner with each other within the team, and with people outside their team, to maximize their resources. They redesigned their approach, and together with the other internal partners, they developed a plan that was more realistic and feasible and led to faster and better results.

Supports Row
In this row, identify the support structures, processes, leadership development activities, networks, and other actions that people need to build the competencies for leading and managing the project. These may also include new tasks or project teams, more active participation from executive team members, or specific leadership and technical development activities to build new skills or implement new technologies and processes.

Communications Row
In this row, list the key milestones, processes, and supports that will help you create effective communications strategies to inform people and engage employees and stakeholders in meaningful conversations throughout the process. This will also help you spot opportunities to reduce duplication and make use of existing corporate and departmental communication methods, products, and processes. It also helps target what needs to be communicated and when and how to approach stakeholders, especially when an organization is undergoing significant change. Mapping your communication activities helps you collaborate more effectively and efficiently by making more visible what, why, how, and when communication needs to happen and who needs to be involved.

In the toolkit in part 2, you will find the Developing a Communications Plan Exercise to help you with this task.

→ The Value of the Master Change Plan

A Master Change Plan can be developed for one specific project or for multiple projects that are occurring simultaneously as part of a larger transformation. In fact, there is a lot of value in doing this exercise with multiple projects and stakeholders to identify synergies, create alignment, and build better focus and capacity to lead and manage change plans. In my work with larger organization-wide change initiatives, I often conduct a Master Change Planning workshop with leaders or teams from the business and corporate services functions, change projects, or initiatives who come together for one day to develop their plans. Usually, the group attends having done some assigned prework prior to the session. Those results are then posted on the wall around the room so everyone can discuss them and learn from each other. The group works to identify and understand the following:

- Are there any patterns that need to be taken into account? For instance, are there any commonalities or synergies among the plans?
- Is anything missing?
- What is unique about each plan that they may not have recognized before?
- What do people observe about the organization's culture? Are there values or customs that need to be honored? Shifted or changed?
- Are there any synergies, dependencies, or interdependencies with people, projects, and deliverables across the organization?
- Are the plans realistic and feasible? Do we agree on the priorities? How about the sequencing of activities and the pace of change?
- Are there ways to work more efficiently and productively by reducing duplication and sharing resources?
- Can we build or strengthen internal partnerships, teamwork, and cross-company collaboration?

I offer the following recommendations to avoid some common pitfalls when using and presenting the Master Change Plan:

1. If you are the type of person who wants to see the preview before the movie, present the plan as a draft

or living document subject to change based on feedback and input, not a fait accompli!

2. Develop a plan to develop the plan. Then be ready to make adjustments as you interact with others and learn about things you may not have previously considered.

3. Keep in mind that the plan is a living document, always subject to change depending on what you learn from your interactions with other people, the environment, and your organization's culture.

4. Be clear about your intentions when presenting your plan. Are you communicating it or presenting it for feedback and input?

5. Watch your language when communicating the plan. For some people, it can be off-putting to hear things like "drive change" or "push change." This sounds like the change is being imposed upon them and leaves no room for collaboration and input.

6. Once you have agreement, focus on your timelines and commitments. Monitor, evaluate, and communicate.

7. Lastly, be accountable and hold each other accountable.

This Master Change Plan process will help you align your project with the larger strategic priorities of your organization. The process provides a reality check on what is realistic to achieve given tight time frames, competing priorities, and finite resources. It helps identify interdependencies and builds collaboration and teamwork across the organization that ultimately results in a stronger shared vision and buy-in for the changes.

In part 2, you will find an exercise called Master Change Plan that will help you go to the next step in developing your plan, advancing your change leadership challenge, and putting these concepts into practice.

→ Putting the LMC Framework and Process Together

You have learned how the LMC Framework is grounded in seven critical principles that need to guide your change plans. These principles are human-centered, universal, and necessary for any change effort to succeed and remain sustainable. To recap, they are:

1. Create a shared purpose, vision, principles, and values.
2. Develop and engage people.
3. Build relationships and foster teamwork and collaboration.
4. Develop the plan to align with strategic priorities and goals.
5. Develop a unified organizational culture to support change.
6. Set up systems, structures, and processes to support the change.
7. Conduct a continuous evaluation of the plan, actions, and impacts.

Meanwhile, you also need to keep your Use-of-Self top of mind at all times. This is your most valuable instrument in your change toolkit. It is constantly at play in the seven principles of the LMC Framework. As leaders, managers, and participants in the LMC Process, we need to pay attention to our intentions and the choices we make about how we show up in the world via our thoughts, our behaviors, and the actions we take to lead and manage ourselves and others throughout the process.

Finally, you learned about the four-stage LMC Process—alignment, integration, action, and renewal. These stages form a comprehensive chronology to achieve the goals of any change effort, large or small. To build lasting culture change, it is vital that the change is well planned and aligned with the organization's priorities. A systems approach that meaningfully engages a critical mass of employees from across your organization and partners with key stakeholders will achieve results that are far greater than the contribution of a single individual or team and that are sustainable over the longer term.

As a tool, the Master Change Plan will help you go beyond the basic tactics so you can build a holistic and integrated plan to successfully lead meaningful change.

Chapter 5

Maximizing
the Power of Teams

Given the complexities of our world, leaders can no longer lead by expertise alone. They must work with and through others, collaborate, and build partnerships both inside their organization and often with external partners, stakeholders, and communities. When we get it right, teams can have a positive influence that permeates quickly to other teams, teams of teams, networks, and communities. Teamwork becomes the glue that bonds people together around the shared purpose and collectively engages their hearts and minds. They reach for and achieve expectations that are far greater than their single contributions. It's magical.

Unfortunately, building and achieving the benefits of teamwork, collaboration, and partnerships is complex. It requires ongoing attention to the interplay of your Use-of-Self as the leader or member of the team, network, or community and your relationships with others to get work done to achieve your shared purpose. If we don't get it right, the reverse of the magic is true. Territoriality, silos, tension, and conflict can quickly spread like a virus and infect teams and the individuals or other teams that they interact with.

Teamwork is an essential ingredient of the LMC Framework and Process. This chapter will delve into how to create and maximize the power of teams, build partnerships, and enhance collaboration across your organization. We will explore the challenges and complexities of building cohesive teams, and look at techniques and strategies to strengthen teamwork, collaboration, and partnerships in the LMC Process.

→ Why Teamwork, Collaboration, and Partnerships?

It would seem unnecessary to answer this question, but I have seen enough organizations fail to maximize the potential of teams, collaborations, and valuable partnerships to solve problems, achieve greater results, and lead meaningful change. For example, do any of these situations sound familiar to you?

- Your organization's senior leadership team is struggling to be more strategic yet is constantly pulled in by operational issues that need attention, so the important work is not getting done.

- You find yourself frequently leaving meetings with no one making a decision. There is no accountability. Ideas are proposed but no one follows up. Everyone thinks the other person "owns" it, whatever it is (decisions, projects, initiatives, and surprisingly, even people!).

- You built a new organizational chart, formed a team, or filled a long-wished-for position on your team, but you're keeping it quiet because you feel others may not accept what you have arranged.

- You and your team must work covertly to deliver on your commitments because of the degree of infighting and resistance coming from others. Deep down you know that you can reach only a certain point and will need to work with other people to achieve the results. You wonder how much longer you and your team can work on your own.

- You are paralyzed or polarized by internal or external politicking and conflict, which are costing money, time, and turnover and putting your project at risk.

- You need to develop your people, a process, or a technology solution but you don't have enough money or resources.

- You are aware that other departments are working on something that you and your team could benefit from or perhaps contribute to achieve a more desirable outcome.

- You are overwhelmed with the expanding number and complexity of people who may be impacted by a change and should be included in your process.

- There are a lot of duplication of work, inefficient processes, and siloed departments in your organization.

- You spend a lot of time in meetings and are constantly playing catch-up on your own work, which is eating into your family and personal time.

- You are living with one foot in the "current world" while working on the "future world."

- You can't do it all and need help.

If you can relate to any one of these situations, you need to call a STOP to what you are doing and begin taking advantage of the much higher productivity that teams and teams of teams can achieve through collaboration and partnering to lead and manage meaningful change.

→ **The Challenges and Complexities of Building Cohesive Teams**

In principle, effective leaders have always achieved results working with and through people. But today's environment demands a far more conscious effort to work through teams, using collaboration and partnership. You may even need to create networks of teams who work collectively at multiple levels within the organization and sometimes even in partnership with external stakeholders and key resources. Leaders today may also need to develop, coach, and provide opportunities for their direct reports, managers, and employees at all levels of the organization to do the same.

This new focus on forming and leveraging teams can be confusing, even if you have led teams in the past. There are now many types of teams at play in our organizations: senior leadership teams, management teams, departmental teams, project teams, cross-company and cross-functional teams, matrixed teams, design teams, transition teams, multicultural teams, multiprofessional and multidisciplinary teams, multinational teams, global teams, virtual teams, closed-ended and open-ended groups, networks, communities of practice, and teams of teams.

Teams can work well and succeed by collaborating with each other, or they can fail by competing against each other. One leader commented to me about the many diverse team cultures that influenced how people worked in teams at his hospital. They had the hallway culture, weekday and weekend staff cultures, military culture, health care professional culture, physician culture, support staff culture, and an "us" (management) versus "them" (everyone else) culture. He was able to create teamwork and collaboration among these groups by focusing on their common purpose to provide the best patient care experience.

In my research, I found that many organizations struggle with creating highly functional, cohesive teams. In chapter 1, I cited the *Change Leadership Challenges* study that I conducted in 2014 among 2,000 participants. The study revealed that regardless of the participant's executive level, expertise, or project, the essential factors for success in their organization were teamwork, collaboration, and working in partnership with others. Many of these 2,000 participants said they found it difficult to build cohesive teams that worked well across the organization and were able to collaborate and build partnerships with strategic and political stakeholders. Some participants had difficulty managing conflict and influencing others when they did not have formal authority or power. Others had difficulty working in virtual teams and building relationships online.

In his book *Overcoming the Five Dysfunctions of a Team*, team expert Patrick Lencioni states that the true measure of a team is that it accomplishes the results it sets out to achieve. To do that on a consistent, ongoing basis, a team must overcome five dysfunctions: absence of trust, fear of conflict, lack of commitment, avoidance of accountability, and inattention to results.[20]

Overcoming these challenges is even more complex when we layer on the frequent changes that often occur in the team's membership. People come and go, others change roles. Such changes can interfere with the team's development on its journey to overcome those five dysfunctions and become what I call a "cohesive team."

→ What Is a Cohesive Team?

In my view, cohesive teams are composed of people who

- are humble and constantly learning and developing their Use-of-Self, understanding their strengths and challenges;
- have a shared understanding of and commitment to the purpose, vision, and strategic direction of the organization and how they support it;
- are passionate about their work and being part of the team;
- understand their accountabilities, roles, and responsibilities;
- trust each other and hold each other accountable;

- can depend on each other when it counts;

- develop and empower their members to collaborate and partner with others to get the work done;

- are curious about each other's business, seek to understand and build on their synergies and interdependencies, and provide support even when they need to be independent;

- have an action plan to guide and evaluate their work; and

- seek to achieve results that far outweigh any single contribution.

→ The Art, Craft, and Science of Developing Cohesive Teams

Developing teams to lead meaningful change cannot be a short-term expectation. It is an iterative process that takes place over the course of the entire lifecycle of a team. It requires understanding and attending to the needs of each member as well as to the entire team's interpersonal and group dynamics as they work together. Team development may need particular attention at various stages of the team's journey, such as when it is just forming, when it is already working together, and when it is going off track and needs to be aligned. Teams can also benefit from development when members join or leave the team. Development can also be useful and effective when teams need to renew their commitment or be challenged to perform at a higher level to move into the next phase of their journey.

The seven guiding principles of the LMC Framework defined in chapter 3 apply to how we develop cohesive teams and the development programs that we design to support them. Principle 2 (develop and engage people) reminds us that the development of the team needs to be grounded in their real work and be multidimensional by including both formal and informal ways of learning that apply to the individual, team, and other levels in the organization. Principle 3 (build relationships and foster teamwork and collaboration) reinforces that we need to look at cohesive teams as a dynamic human system that is constantly changing and impacted by their interactions with each other and their internal and external environments. Teams are also influenced by their members' individual Use-of-Self and the impact they each have as they interact.

Developing cohesive teams throughout the organization starts with the top team. It sets the tone and models the mindsets, values, and behaviors of teamwork, collaboration, and partnerships. The top team can have a positive cascading impact that permeates into those managers, supervisors, and employees whom they lead and manage across the organization. If teamwork at the top is not aligned, the opposite is true: it can have a negative cascading impact that can erode trust and create tensions and conflict. These same cascading impacts exist with leaders and teams at other levels of the organization.

We know that change is not a linear process. This also applies to how we develop teams. In my experience, creating cohesive teams and maximizing their power is an art, craft, and science, requiring a multifaceted and multilayered approach. An example of the art of team building is the paradox that one cannot focus on developing the team leader in isolation from the team, nor can one develop the team without paying attention to each member's impact on the others or on the larger human systems that they work with and in, such as those they partner with and serve. In effect, you need to think in terms of a systemic approach that simultaneously and collectively aims to develop the individuals, their interrelationships, and their group dynamics working together as a team. This complexity of perspectives and thoughtful attention to the entire canvas thus becomes as much an art form as a master artist might employ, stepping back at times to see the big picture or zooming in at other times to look at the details.

An example of the craft of team building is the need to create a healthy team culture that pays attention to the emotional health and well-being of the team while not abandoning its goals. You do this by balancing the expression of emotions that may arise within the team with the practical work that must be done. Neither can be disregarded if both the individual and the team are to thrive, not just survive.

As for the science of team building, cohesive teams also need hard-nosed mechanics to help them be successful. These include things like a team charter, organizational structures, decision-making processes, and tools and supports to advance their work, lead and manage change, and enhance their learning and development. Developing an evaluation process is also critical and should include a needs assessment, a baseline measure of performance, and ways to monitor the individual and the team's performance throughout the LMC Process. This helps the team understand when and why they are being successful or when they need to correct or adjust their approach.

To launch any change effort with a goal of maximizing the greater power of teams, I recommend forming a design team composed of a mix of internal and external expertise. This could include both internal and external coaches, trainers, consultants, and partners whose role will be to design, monitor, support, and evaluate the team-building efforts. At the same time, I also recommend that once other teams are formed, involving each team to co-develop their own development plan ensures their commitment to the strategies of change laid out by the design team. Each team can thus take part in developing the more specific tactics that are relevant and grounded in their real work, address their needs, and help them achieve meaningful results.

→ The Use of Theoretical Group Models and Assessments

There are many well-researched models of team development and psychometric assessments to formally diagnose and assess individual, team, and organizational development and performance. It is beyond the scope of this book to explain these models, but I do recommend understanding and using one of these team development models and psychometric assessments to provide benchmarking and data points during the change effort. These can help create an objective, shared understanding of the strengths, challenges, and development opportunities to improve individual, leadership, team, and organizational performance. However, these assessments need to consider the context of your workplace and be aligned with your goals and objectives. For this reason, it is valuable to include external experts in the early design team meetings so as to orient its members to the theoretical and psychometric tools that can assist with the team's development. This knowledge can then be cascaded down to the internal team members who will be co-developing their tactics for the solutions, techniques, and supports that will help them perform at their best.

If you do not hire external resources, it is important to develop your own formal leadership and team assessments and pulse checks to monitor the needs, performance, and impacts of individuals and teams. It is useful to conduct these assessments at several critical milestones along the team's journey so you can get a sense of whether their development is moving forward or is blocked. At a minimum, here are some questions that are worth asking individual leaders and team members to assess informally how well they are working as a cohesive team to lead meaningful change:

1. What do you need to be at your best as a leader or member of this team?
2. Are you achieving your desired impact and meaningful results? If so, why? If not, why not?

3. What is helping or hindering your success?
4. What actions do you need to take as an individual team member or collectively as a team to be more effective?
5. What additional supports do you or the team need to be successful?

→ Ten LMC Guidelines for Developing Cohesive Teams

Regardless of whichever theory of group and team development you subscribe to, it can be useful to have a formalized and concrete set of baseline standards for the team's process, procedures, and interpersonal and team dynamics. In my work with organizations, I have devised ten guidelines for cohesive teamwork. Adopt or adapt them as needed throughout the lifecycle of your team. They can also be used when you need to coordinate teams of teams. Effectively, these guidelines are the basis for what I call a "team charter" that members agree to abide by.

1. Establish the values and behaviors that team members will hold each other accountable for. These may include, and are not limited to, specific statements on trust, respect, collaboration, and communication.

2. Establish norms that help everyone accomplish their work. These norms can be as simple as agreeing to start and finish meetings on time, putting personal phones away, clarifying expectations on what is an emergency, and acknowledging that people are or are not expected to respond to a boss or each other 24/7. Establish boundaries so you will know what is a confidential conversation to be kept within the team, and what is for general knowledge and communication.

3. Seek to understand the relationships, responsibilities, and accountabilities within the team and each member's relationships with other teams, stakeholders, partners, and the rest of the organization and community.

4. Pay attention to each person's Use-of-Self and the impacts they have on others, and on you.

5. Develop a "safe enough and relevant space" that promotes a healthy emotional climate in the team and gets work done. This requires being aware of and managing your own emotions and, at the same time, developing ways to notice and respect others as they express theirs.

6. Agree on a structure for meetings. For example, prepare an agenda with objectives, responsibilities, and outcomes for each topic. Take minutes and assign accountabilities for follow-up.

7. Put in place a "check-in and check-out" process in meetings to ask how people are feeling and what they are thinking when the team first comes together and again when the meeting wraps up. Notice how people are showing up: Are they fully present? Are they paying attention? Look not just at what people say, but also at their body language. Are they excited, passionate, deflated, struggling, angry, confused, or in conflict? This checking process provides information about the emotional climate and mood of the team.

8. Be clear about your decision-making process. State when you are making a decision, making a recommendation, or tabling something for further discussion.

9. Include communication as a standing item at the end of your meetings. This will help you develop key messages about what needs to be communicated and to whom following your meeting. You may not have solutions or a final decision, and that is sometimes okay. This discussion will help you be clear about your process and the key messages that will help you speak as one team, with one voice.

10. Share and celebrate success at key stages and milestones of the LMC Process. Use these as an opportunity to thank and acknowledge people for their hard work and shine a light on the meaningful results they achieved. This is also an opportunity to reflect on the way people worked to achieve the results; this speaks to the culture shifts, new mindsets, and behaviors that you want to continue.

→ Case Study: Building Teamwork in a Complex Environment

Here is an example of how one leader (who had been a participant in my Change Leadership Essentials program) applied these LMC guidelines in his approach to building a cohesive team in a complex environment.

John (his name has been changed) was a director responsible for developing and installing a new financial management system for his company. The executive management team had authorized him to develop a new system that would streamline, standardize, and integrate the company's business processes into one system to ensure the financials were tracked and accurate so that the company could grow and deliver plans to the market with confidence.

John assumed the role as project leader to oversee and implement this work. However, he did not have formal authority over the team he was to lead. The company had a matrix structure, so team members working on the project still reported to their functional managers. John's team also worked with their respective functional and extended teams to provide the necessary inputs and implement the project plans. In addition, John worked with external consultants who provided expertise that the organization did not have internally.

John's new role was a development move for him and a new leadership challenge. He had to lead this team and a team of teams, plus convince political stakeholders to agree on and commit to a shared vision by influencing and coaching them. At the same time, he was responsible for delivering the system on time and on budget. It was a critical project, and the company's success depended on it.

John knew this project would require a significant culture shift, not only as they designed and built the system, but also when it was implemented throughout the organization. The planning, accounting, and management team members who were part of the project team had to rethink the way they developed their financial plans and measured outcomes. They were asked to use new software to support a new planning process that would be less flexible and more rigorous. It would also require alignment between some new divisions.

John knew he had to form the right team, build collaboration, and form partnerships to be successful. However, he was not ready for the degree of resistance and lack of teamwork he faced. Firstly, there was co-opitition (cooperation and competition) between the departments. The functional and extended teams were territorial about protecting their resources, including their people and budgets. They also had long-standing relationships with suppliers and partners that they did not want to change. Legacy systems were not being fully used, which indicated greater efficiencies were needed. At the same time, there was an organizational review underway that created uncertainty about future work and job security.

To add to the mix, the external consultants were competing with the internal people. They acted as "the experts" and did not take time to fully understand or respect the internal knowledge and expertise, nor the issues and concerns raised by those internal team members. All in all, this project was highly political, yet the company's future depended on it. John had a mandate to work together as a team to develop and implement this solution. The plan was the easy part; building a cohesive team was harder.

Here is how John began to handle the challenge. The culture shift required the team to be more transparent about the project plan and expected outcomes. They learned that they needed to communicate more frequently. They also conducted a stakeholder analysis every two weeks to determine who was onside and what else they needed to do to help people have confidence and participate in the project plan. This process helped the team work better together. It also modeled for themselves and the rest of the organization the values and behaviors of teamwork, collaboration, and partnerships between the people on the team and their departments.

They held working sessions focused on change leadership and change management with both the external consultants and their internal teams. This created a common language and opportunities to learn about each member and their expertise, strengths, issues, and concerns. They coached each other and their extended teams. They shared wise practices and communicated about how they were using the diverse knowledge, skill sets, and experiences of the people involved to inform the development of the new system and the process to get them there. Their approach required each of the team members to be a leader of change and, at the same time, manage the plan. This helped break down the silos, created alignment, and strengthened teamwork and collaboration across the organization.

In those sessions, they also developed a Master Change Plan that helped them align the project plan with other initiatives simultaneously underway in the organization. This also helped the project team to get the approvals they needed from various political stakeholders and to make use of the work of other teams such that they reduced costs and time, shared the vision for change, and got support for the project across the entire organization. In the end, John was able to complete the project on time and within budget, which he knew would not have been possible without the degree of teamwork he had been able to assemble.

Chapter 6

←——————→

Tools to Foster Teamwork, Collaboration, and Partnerships in Leading Meaningful Change

In this chapter, I will walk you through several key activities, shown in Figure 7, that I use at various times during the LMC Process to develop people, create cohesive teams, and foster collaboration across an organization when leading and managing change. These exercises can be scaled up or down to meet the needs of your organization and used at any stage of the LMC Process. Consider these techniques and tools as a buffet that you can select from to customize your own team development plan. Choose the ones that best fit your needs and that will help you keep your teams moving in a healthy and positive direction.

As you will note, these practices are all grounded in the LMC Framework discussed in chapter 3. Here they are again as a reminder:

1. Create a shared purpose, vision, principles, and values.
2. Develop and engage people.
3. Build relationships and foster teamwork and collaboration.
4. Develop the plan to align with strategic priorities and goals.
5. Develop a unified organizational culture to support change.

6. Set up systems, structures, and processes to support the change.

7. Conduct a continuous evaluation of the plan, actions, and impacts.

→ Stage 1: Alignment Activities

As discussed in chapter 4, stage 1 focuses on aligning the change plan with the strategy and priorities of the entire organization. This work starts with forming a design team whose role is to determine the themes, patterns, successes, challenges, and impacts that need to be considered in the program design and next steps. To foster highly functional design and leadership teams, I often conduct a series of checkpoint meetings with leaders and the design team before and after each of the key milestones. In this process, we seek feedback on individual and team development and performance, as well as evaluate their effectiveness in moving the change plan forward. We also conduct more formal working sessions with the leadership team, and depending on the size of the organization, these may extend to inviting the next layer of leadership in the organization to join in. These working sessions are designed to create a shared vision, understanding, and commitment to support the change, and develop what will become the guiding principles and the plans for change. These sessions are also designed to align the leadership teams, clarify their roles and responsibilities, provide them with tools and supports to lead and manage the change, and assess their interpersonal and group dynamics to determine the strategies and next steps for the LMC Process.

One activity that I often recommend to the design team is an exercise called Envisioning Success. This is a creative exercise you can use to build and enhance teamwork and collaboration, especially during the early stages of a team's formation. The exercise projects people into the future and asks them to look back to the present and say what they

Figure 7 **LMC** Tools and Techniques for Building Teamwork, Collaboration, and Partnerships

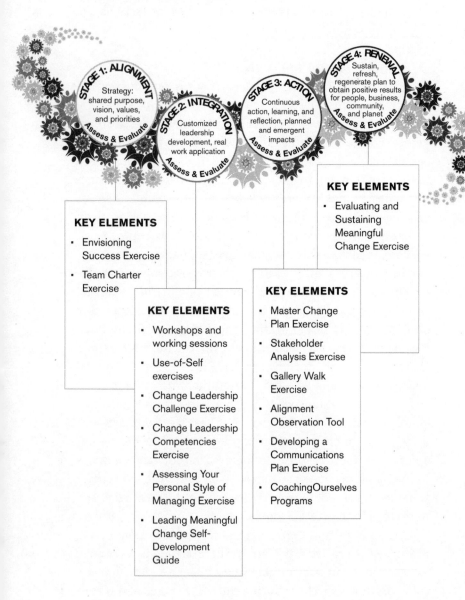

STAGE 1: ALIGNMENT
Strategy: shared purpose, vision, values, and priorities
Assess & Evaluate

STAGE 2: INTEGRATION
Customized leadership development, real work application
Assess & Evaluate

STAGE 3: ACTION
Continuous action, learning, and reflection, planned and emergent impacts
Assess & Evaluate

STAGE 4: RENEWAL
Sustain, refresh, regenerate plan to obtain positive results for people, business, community, and planet
Assess & Evaluate

KEY ELEMENTS

- Envisioning Success Exercise
- Team Charter Exercise

KEY ELEMENTS

- Workshops and working sessions
- Use-of-Self exercises
- Change Leadership Challenge Exercise
- Change Leadership Competencies Exercise
- Assessing Your Personal Style of Managing Exercise
- Leading Meaningful Change Self-Development Guide

KEY ELEMENTS

- Master Change Plan Exercise
- Stakeholder Analysis Exercise
- Gallery Walk Exercise
- Alignment Observation Tool
- Developing a Communications Plan Exercise
- CoachingOurselves Programs

KEY ELEMENTS

- Evaluating and Sustaining Meaningful Change Exercise

←—— Continuous cycles of evaluation to measure results and impacts ——→

did to achieve success. This encourages people to develop a vision of the actual work they need to do to realize their goals. This exercise also tends to bring out the team's passions, talents, and their shared values.

Envisioning Success Exercise

There are two options to conduct this exercise. One is for those who prefer a module in a workshop, and the other is for those who want something more experiential in the moment. Here is the setup and questions for each approach.

Option 1: Envisioning Success Group Workshop
As the facilitator of this exercise, you can set up the team or groups with flip charts and use the following directions:

1. Begin by asking the group to imagine that it is [*select a future date, years from now*]. You and your team are very happy and excited about your achievements. Find words and/or images to describe what you are feeling, seeing, and hearing as you observe people functioning in the new world (this could be the implementation of the changes that you are working on, a culture shift, a new technology system, new business process, etc.).

2. Ask the group: What are you seeing that is different from when you began this change journey for your customers, clients, employees, leaders, stakeholders, and community?

3. On the flip chart, have each member list the actions taken to achieve their objectives. Prioritize and sequence those actions.

4. Have the group present and share their results.

Option 2: Envisioning Success Team Interview
In this exercise, set up the room so people are sitting in a circle or around the table. Place yourself as the facilitator at

one end of the table so you can see the whole team, or sit inside the circle so you can see everyone. Then introduce yourself as if you are an interviewer writing an article for a magazine, newspaper, or awards ceremony that is relevant to the audience. As people speak, take notes on a pad of paper. Don't use a flip chart to record the answers, as this will become a distraction.

Below are some questions to get you started interviewing your team. Ask these questions as though it is two years from now. For example, if you are doing this exercise on July 10, 2020, and your project implementation date is July 2022, say something like, "I'm excited to meet with you today. It's July 2022, two years after we first met, when you were just beginning this project. Reflecting back over your last two years..."

1. What did you do to become a cohesive change team and deliver these amazing results?
2. What values and principles did you use to guide your decisions and work?
3. How did you organize yourselves?
4. What was your contribution to the team's success?
5. What was your contribution to the project's success?
6. What did you do to create a shared vision and alignment with the key stakeholders that you needed for success?
7. How do you measure success?

Here are some hints to help you conduct this option for the exercise:

· Ask everyone to speak as if they are already in the future looking into the past (in other words, they should speak in past tense).

· Ensure everyone has a chance to participate. If they don't speak up on their own, you can ask them individually to tell you what they did to contribute to the team's success. You may hear something like,

"I'm really proud of the work we did as a leadership team to implement the new organizational structure across the corporation. As the director of technology and member of the leadership team, I worked closely with Jane, the manager from human resources, to design a process to develop a new structure in my area that was aligned with the new corporate structure. This was a learning opportunity for me. Jane's coaching, tools, and supports helped me to develop new skills and work more effectively as a member of the leadership team while we designed and implemented the new structure in my area and across the corporation."

- Encourage everyone to describe what they did using action verbs. You may need to gently correct the first speakers to answer this way.

- Remind people to speak about what they did *individually* to work with others and how they supported the team's work. Sometimes people default to "we," and it may seem a bit awkward at first to speak about themselves, but doing this ultimately helps people ground their vision of actions in ways that are realistic about their choices, sphere of control, and influence.

- If you know of particular tensions, conflicts, or obstacles, ask the team, "How did you overcome the obstacle or resolve the conflict?"

- If you know the team members, try to continue the thread of the conversation so you can build on their ideas and pull out the specific skills, expertise, interdependencies, and synergies that relate to the objectives and the plan that you've been working on.

Team Charter Exercise

The Envisioning Success Exercise can also be customized to develop a team charter for leading meaningful change.

Here are the elements that are valuable to include in an LMC team charter:

1. Purpose, vision, mission, and strategy
2. Organizational culture: structure, formal and informal systems, and policies and procedures
3. Relationships: values, mindsets, behaviors, skills, knowledge, expertise, norms, and interpersonal and team dynamics, especially when dealing with conflict
4. Governance and accountabilities: roles and responsibilities, decision making, approvals, and advising, consulting, and engaging others
5. Communications
6. Individual and team development plans
7. Evaluation of impacts and performance: measures of success for the team, people, business, community, and planet

→ Stage 2: Integration Activities

In stage 2, the focus is on developing customized leadership development interventions, techniques, and tools that are grounded in real work. To foster teamwork throughout this stage, I work with the design team to create and deliver a variety of what I call Change Leadership Essentials modules that can take many forms: customized workshops, team working sessions, online work, self-assessments, and other formats. These modules and activities are designed to provide a foundation for what is needed to lead and manage change.

This work begins with understanding the Use-of-Self as discussed in chapters 1 and 2 and may include exercises on Use-of-Self, leadership and team assessments, and other activities that help leaders see themselves in action and witness the impact that they have on others and vice versa. These modules are a great way to help teams understand their strengths and use their challenges as development opportunities. These modules result in a better understanding of the senior leadership and design team's change leadership competencies. The modules also provide leaders and team members with new tools and techniques to help themselves and their teams be their best selves as leaders, managers, consultants, service providers, coaches, and mentors throughout the change process.

Change Leadership Challenge Exercise

One of the key exercises I often use in this stage (though it can be used in other stages as well) is the Change Leadership Challenge Exercise. This exercise can be completed by the design team, leadership team, or individual project teams. It is designed to help them reflect on their real work and identify the key areas that they need to work on to be successful. This follows the precept of the LMC Framework to "use work, not make work."

The Change Leadership Challenge Exercise is started as an initial reflection on the participants' project, but it then becomes a living document that they work on throughout the change effort and LMC Process. Participants can choose to work on a project as a team or on their own, but it must be supported by their managers, done within their actual flow of work and within their span of control, and aligned with the strategic priorities. They are invited to draw on the support and resources of other participants and their extended teams to help shape and advance their projects.

At key milestones, and especially at the conclusion of the program, participants share their results and reflections on their learning and accomplishments in a presentation and discussion with their senior leadership team and other invited guests. In this way, this project helps break down silos, creates stronger alignment, and facilitates knowledge sharing among team members. It also is effective in helping the teams to coach upward.

This exercise is also a key tool to help the design team better understand each member's needs for development and obtain a baseline assessment of the themes and patterns that need to be addressed throughout the program. It also helps them focus on the specific tools, techniques, and supports they need to help leaders advance their work.

Additional Stage 2 Exercises in Part 2: Toolkit

Change Leadership Competencies Exercise

This is another exercise that I ask team members to do. You will find this activity in the part 2 toolkit. It can be used throughout the change process to assess how well you and your team are doing as you lead and manage change.

Assessing Your Personal Style of Managing Exercise

As discussed, the LMC Process views team building as an art, a craft, and a science. In part 2, you will find an exercise to help you assess your personal style of managing in terms of this notion of art, craft, and science. This exercise can also be applied to your team and generate rich discussion about your team's preferences and the impact you are having as you lead and manage change.

Leading Meaningful Change Self-Development Guide

This guide is designed for leaders to complete on their own to create their personal leadership development plan. It contains exercises to develop a personal vision and purpose, reflect on their priorities, and identify the actions and supports they need to lead meaningful change.

→ Stage 3: Action Activities and the Master Change Plan Work

As you recall, stage 3 focuses on having team members develop a Master Change Plan that aligns their work with other initiatives in the organization. As a key exercise at this stage to support the sense of team and build on the potential for collaboration and partnership, I suggest that design team members and/or individual project teams present their department or unit change plans to each other, seeking feedback and input. This often helps team members discover new synergies and interdependencies they can explore with others, deepening their understanding of how to engage and partner with others and even instigating specific collaborations. This process helps them advance their plans, maximize efficiencies, and make use of other activities and resources in the organization that they may not have previously considered. Themes, patterns, and organizational culture issues often surface, leading to further discussion and negotiation. This exercise also helps team members check their expectations about the pace of change and align their work with other projects and the larger organizational strategic plan and priorities.

As part of this process, participants may also conduct a stakeholder analysis that they then monitor throughout the program. This analysis deepens people's understanding of stakeholder concerns, issues, and needs. It helps the team develop strategies to engage people and work through resistance. To enhance this process, you can also add the Gallery Walk Exercise and Alignment Observation Tool, both described below.

Gallery Walk Exercise

The Gallery Walk Exercise is based on work that I have done with clients and have written about in an article called "Discovering the Magic of Culture Shifts."[21] This exercise can be used to support the Master Change Plan Exercise, or it can be used independently as a strategic or operational planning exercise. The origin of the exercise relates to the struggles that people often experience in times of change about how much of their plans to disclose to peers and superiors due to political and power conflicts, or their desire to protect their limited resources of people, time, and budget. The Gallery Walk Exercise is designed to facilitate an easy, informal conversation about the plans, share innovative ideas, identify synergies, and identify opportunities to partner, collaborate, or address issues.

To do this exercise, first enlarge each team's change plan to poster size and hang the plans on the wall like artwork in a gallery. Ask team members to walk around the room in silence, review each plan, and write their feedback, questions, suggestions, and recommendations right on the posters. Then ask each leader to give a brief presentation about their own plan while addressing the feedback written on the posters.

This process surfaces, in a very natural way, the important and distinctive work of each team or department and the many synergies, interdependencies, and common challenges across all plans. The sharing often reinforces the need and value for teamwork, collaboration, and partnership.

The Gallery Walk also reveals where people and projects are in the change process. Typically, not everyone is at the same stage of developing or implementing their plans. This process reveals concrete examples, ways to create alignment if it wasn't there before, as well as ideas to synchronize or adjust the pace or sequencing of the changes, or help people along who may be struggling or putting your own project at risk.

Note: Some teams prefer to send the plans to participants or the design team ahead of the workshop so that they can complete the exercise as part of their preparation and come to the Gallery Walk with a summary of the themes and patterns that may have surfaced in their preliminary review. If you choose this option, I recommend presenting the summary after the workshop participants have done their exercise. This will prevent any bias or leading in one direction or the other.

Alignment Observation Tool

Table 6 is the grid for another valuable exercise I use to break down silos, identify synergies, align people and plans, make necessary adjustments, and identify new opportunities to

Table 6 Alignment Observation Tool

Observations and insights on strategic priorities	Opportunities for alignment, synergies, efficiencies, partnerships, and collaboration	Resources that I need to share or use to build capacity and focus for success	Strategies and actions that intersect, are interdependent, or are dependent on some of our deliverables	Ideas that I will use in my work

Sample Filled-Out Alignment Observation Tool				
Observations and insights	**Opportunities**	**Resources**	**Strategies and actions**	**Ideas**
☐ Service excellence ☑ Organizational effectiveness ☐ Employee engagement	HR [human resources] has recruitment strategies to plan, organize, process, and administer applications that we can use in our recruitment of new hires	Our project team, the plan, timelines, and deliverables and the research that we have collected to inform our plan	The team needs to meet with HR to fully understand the process, efficiencies, processing time, how to ensure accuracy, and how to maintain the high level of satisfaction that we currently have with the applicants	Recruitment strategies, structure, and process in HR and the technology system

collaborate and partner. I often do this exercise as an adjunct to the Gallery Walk. In addition to writing their observations on the posters for public display, each person has a copy of this grid and uses it as their private diary to take notes as they walk through the gallery. These notes can be used as reminders of ideas they'd like to use, or to record feedback to be shared after the Gallery Walk. In addition, the design team can use their notes to conduct a preliminary scan of the plans for their working session.

To do this exercise, reproduce the template shown in Table 6. The white space below each heading is where participants will write their notes. The sample filled-out form below Table 6 shows what one participant wrote about a project dealing with service excellence in one of my client organizations.

Participants can use their notes to talk with the other workshop participants about their observations and the strategies, actions, and ideas that may have surfaced during the Gallery Walk. They can also take their notes away and incorporate them in their own planning.

→ Stages 1 to 4: Intersession Activities

There are a wealth of activities and interventions you can use throughout the course of the change effort between the stage 1 kickoff meetings of the design team and the final phase of the LMC Process. These can be delivered as separate topics in a workshop format, or combined to form a program taking a day or longer depending on your needs, the size of the teams, and the complexity of your organization. For instance, if you are the CEO of a small organization, you may want to do a workshop based on the LMC Framework to reflect on your practice of leading and managing change to understand what you are doing well and where you may want to improve. If you are working with a larger organization, you may want to use the design team to help coordinate and customize this program to meet your needs.

CoachingOurselves Programs

Another highly effective tool I recommend to use between workshops or as a stand-alone process is CoachingOurselves (CO). This unique approach to management and leadership development was created by Henry Mintzberg and Phil LeNir. I have been using CO for many years to build a shared mindset about leading and managing change, specifically to generate meaningful conversations that help people reflect on their own experiences and learn from and coach each other.

The CO approach is designed for small self-directed learning groups of typically six to eight participants who meet for 80 minutes and learn about a leadership or management topic that is relevant to them and that they can apply in their real work. There are over 80 topics to choose from that can be packaged into three to six topics focused on themes like leading change or managing to address the participant and organization's learning and development needs. The CO approach is scalable, as it can be used in small teams of six to eight participants or with multiple teams in larger workshops. CO can also be a stand-alone program to build support for learning and development as a community of practice, a team of teams, or a network across the organization.

To conduct a CO program in some client organizations, we form teams of people who do not normally work together in their typical day-to-day work. Having a mix of people from various parts of the organization helps them gain a wider understanding of other parts of the business and build relationships as they go through the course materials and discuss the topic. They also learn that their organizational challenges are not usually unique to themselves, but are sometimes experienced by others and are representative of their organizational culture. CO programs, when implemented with cross-company teams, can be very effective in strengthening multidisciplinary, diverse teamwork and cross-industry learning. They have often surfaced natural ways to partner and collaborate.

Throughout a CO program, the learning team or network meets regularly between formal working sessions for further informal discussions. The themes and patterns that emerge during these discussions can be tracked and shared with the larger group during the formal working sessions. This helps the larger community develop a shared understanding of the learning team's journey and to learn from each other. Their reflections and discoveries also inform the ongoing program design and their work going forward. This has helped people to understand the culture shifts that are required, leading to faster and deeper adoption of the changes.

→ Stage 4: Renewal Activities

Evaluations are done throughout the LMC Process, but in this stage, they are vital for measuring, monitoring, and evaluating the team's learning, development, and impact. Stage 4 evaluations help the team reflect on their accomplishments and the success of culture shifts. The evaluation process at this time can include surveys, self-assessments, face-to-face interviews, online pulse surveys, and many other formats that help assess the team's effectiveness and performance in leading the change.

An effective evaluation process results in rich and meaningful data to help the team understand how they are leading the changes, what they are doing well, and where they need to change or renew their plans. The evaluation process should also analyze the objectives of the change and the development program, as well as the effectiveness of the strategies, tools, and techniques used for development. These too may need adjustments along the way. The evaluation process should be conducted at key milestones of the LMC Process.

In part 2, you will find a sample of the Evaluating and Sustaining Meaningful Change Exercise, which includes an assessment that the team can do to measure how well they are leading culture shifts at each stage of the LMC Process.

At this stage, you can also do an online self-assessment survey of the change leadership competencies mentioned earlier and the team's values. The results should be shared with the team at each stage or milestone so they can validate the findings and together decide on their next steps.

→ Case Study: Using CoachingOurselves to Build Skills in Leading a Change Effort

Here is an example of how Dr. Cynthia Smith, dean of the School of Health and Human Services (HHS) at Camosun College in Victoria, British Columbia, used CoachingOurselves (CO) as part of her work with the LMC Process to develop a team of leaders and managers in support of a transformational change in HHS.

HHS offers more than 15 programs, including a joint degree, a post-degree diploma, certificates, and university transfer courses. With buildings on two campuses, HHS serves over 1,000 students and employs 100 faculty and staff, mostly in the newly finished Alex & Jo Campbell Centre for Health and Wellness.

These HHS programs fall into six departments, each with a chair who leads faculty development and the financial and program management of the department. Faculty take on the chair role for a three-year term, with the possibility of renewal. Faculty are content experts who teach in their discipline. They usually do not have any specific management training, yet having taken on a department leadership role, they are interested in gaining these skills. The college offers both teaching and leadership training as well as training specific to human resources and financial and business processes, but does not offer training on management skills per se. In addition to meeting the needs of faculty performing the chair role, leadership and management skills were especially relevant at this time, as the college had a new strategic plan with which HHS needed to align. These strategic priorities would result in significant changes that the team of department chairs would have to lead and manage.

In addition, the college was undertaking the greatest change in its history with the construction of a new building to house all HHS programs on another campus. This would entail the movement of HHS faculty, staff, and equipment to the new campus, and the movement of other college departments to fill the space vacated by HHS at the Lansdowne Campus. A plan to support the move to a new location was in progress at the time of the CO program, and the same team of department chairs would also be leading and managing these strategic priorities.

Recognizing the need for management training, Cynthia, along with her HHS leadership team composed of the six chairs and two senior administrative support personnel, participated in a CO program designed to provide them with an opportunity to build their understanding of and skills in leading and managing change. The details of their program were as follows.

Objectives
The objectives for the HHS CO program were to

1. provide the HHS leadership group an opportunity to reflect on their practice of leading and managing;
2. learn concepts and tools to create a shared mindset and advance their ability to lead and manage in the School of Health and Human Services; and
3. strengthen the leadership group's ability to work together as a senior leadership team.

Table 7 shows an overview of what we referred to as the HHS Leadership Group Development Program, which was based on the LMC Framework and Process, along with several of the LMC activities discussed in this chapter and three CO courses.

This program was designed to develop the HHS leadership team in real time, improving their competencies as they went through it. The program took place over a nine-month period and was led by a design team who provided oversight and coordination of the needs assessment, the three CO sessions, the evaluation process, a train-the-trainer module for CO, and other activities. The design team was composed of Cynthia, the dean, the associate dean, a program manager, and me as an external consultant and coach.

First, as shown at the top of this chart, the design group began with strategic and operational alignment work. This was led and managed by Cynthia and the chairs. Given the academic culture, we also needed to ensure the CO program development process was collaborative, was built on wise practices, and, as much as possible, used evidence-based research.

Table 7 **Overview of HHS Leadership Group Development Program**

Alignment Process

Vision: Inspiring life-changing learning, conducting a strategic planning session, aligning the nursing department, planning for the move to a new building, and delivering the HHS programs.

CO Launch	CO Topic 1	CO Topic 2	CO Topic 3	ExperienceChange Workshop
Envisioning Success Exercise Leadership team needs assessment	*Managing on the Planes of Information, People, and Action* by Henry Mintzberg	*Strategic Blindspots* by Estelle Métayer	*Probing into Culture* by Edgar Schein	HHS leadership group and program leaders

Learning in Action

Simply Managing by Henry Mintzberg, coaching, readings, tools, and resources to advance personal, team, and program development

Management Happenings

CoachingOurselves Evaluation Process

Monthly design team meetings to reflect on CO process, impact, and topic selection

CoachingOurselves online evaluation, train-the-trainer development

In the next phase, we launched the CO program with an overview of CO, the LMC Envisioning Success Exercise (discussed earlier in the chapter), and a needs assessment to ensure the program elements and topics were relevant for the chairs and would meet the needs of the group. Following their approval, we provided a list of CO topics, and the group selected three they found to be most relevant given their work as the leadership group. Change management was especially important at this time, so they selected the topics shown in Table 7 to gain an understanding of managing, culture change, and learning skills to work with faculty.

The leadership group then met every two months to complete each CO topic, followed by a full-day workshop called ExperienceChange (explained in chapter 4) that was custom-designed for this leadership group and their program leaders.

In the next phase, Learning in Action, which took place between CO sessions, the chairs read the book *Simply Managing* by Henry Mintzberg and discussed the concepts at the start of each CO session. Additional coaching and resources were provided so people could advance their individual learning and development. Some of the chairs also used these supports with their respective teams and reported on this during the Management Happenings (debriefing) portion of the CO session.

Finally, a critical element of the program was evaluating the process. The evaluation focused on alignment, leadership, actions, and impact (Figure 8).

Figure 8 Evaluation Framework for Leading, Managing, and Inspiring Healthy Community

The evaluations consisted of several elements. In addition to the content from the Management Happenings and feedback received at the end of each CO session, we administered an online survey at the end of the third CO session. The survey was designed to assess the participants' satisfaction with the CO topics and process, and the growth of the team's change leadership competencies and progress toward the program objectives. We also asked open-ended questions to assess their top three takeaways and recommendations for improvement. The results were used to inform the team's next steps.

As the figure represents, the leadership group's goal was to develop a shared vision and meaning of what it is to lead, manage, and inspire a healthy community in HHS. The results revealed that, in terms of leadership, the participants were very grateful for the learning experience and approach. The process, tools, and resources were relevant for their work (alignment) and a good investment for them as individual leaders, as the HHS leadership group, and for their teams.

In regards to impact, in terms of developing their change leadership competencies, team members said that they were still developing skills and would like more clarity on the direction for their department going forward. They agreed they wanted to continue developing as a leadership group. At the same time, they felt that they were equipped with effective practices, tools, and supports for their own learning and development. They wanted more support in developing strategies to lead and manage change in their department and within the school, given the move to the new campus.

On that basis, for actions, the leadership team decided to add the Experiencing Change Workshop, which included the ExperienceChange simulation described earlier, an overview of wise practices, and a toolkit to lead and manage change. They included program leaders from all HHS programs in this workshop. The leadership team also expressed a desire to expand CO courses to their program leaders and continue the process as a leadership group. They were fully engaged in the change process.

By the end of the program, and based on the results, the leadership group began working on the next phase, which would focus on cascading the CO process to the program leaders. They also designed a train-the-trainer process to assist them in leading and managing this process in their respective programs.

This case study shows how a CO program strongly reinforces the elements of the LMC Framework and Process. The CO courses helped the leadership group reflect on their shared experiences, strengthened their ability to work together as a senior leadership team, and gave them concepts and tools that helped them create a shared mindset and advance their leadership and management practices so they could lead meaningful change for HHS.

→ Case Study: Using the LMC Framework and Process in a Small Not-for-Profit

The principles and practices of the LMC Process can also be self-taught and used to build teams in small organizations and on short-term projects. To illustrate this, I would like to share a case study dealing with a not-for-profit theater group. While this example takes place in a non-corporate business environment, it serves as an example of how not-for-profit organizations can equally use the concepts and tools of this book in their work.

The case begins with an actor, Steve Walters, who had a germ of an idea for a play based on the musical *Camelot*, but told in pantomime—thus he called it *Camelot the Panto*. Steve did not originally consider himself a director, but he knew he needed a team effort to make the play happen. He began by approaching two experienced directors to talk about his idea, only to discover that they had no interest in the play. Disappointed, he hesitated. Something held him back. For many years he had acted in the community theater, but he had no experience directing.

But then one day, by chance, he was in the theater and saw the executive director walking toward him. He had chills as he told the executive director his idea. There was a lull in the conversation, but then they both said "pantomime," and they automatically connected. Steve said it was electrifying; he had found an enthusiastic executive director who shared his vision and supported him to direct it.

Steve quickly committed to the project despite knowing that it would be a huge undertaking. At one point, however, he was overwhelmed with budgets and working with designers, technical staff, and community partners. While putting together a proposal for the production, he asked himself, "What have I done?" It was new territory for him, and more than he had expected. But he dug deep and believed so strongly in the project, and in the theater team, that he persevered.

He soon found that his enthusiasm was contagious. People who originally hadn't committed to his idea rallied behind him, as did many new supporters. They became a core base of the cast, and as a bonus, it turned out that many had the pantomime skills the play would need.

He then put his vision into practice. He secured approvals and funding for the production and developed a set of guiding principles that would shape how he would lead a meaningful change in the way his play would be produced at this not-for-profit theater company. His changes were as follows:

1. The audition process would be fair and transparent for everyone.
2. The cast needed to have the ability to work in a team and the desire to learn about pantomime.
3. People would be selected based on the best fit for the role and play. Experience with pantomime was not necessary.
4. This would be a learning experience for everyone. He would teach people if they were new to pantomime.
5. Everyone would be held accountable to speak up and contribute their ideas and experiences.
6. They would have fun!

He then wrote the play according to his vision and did not accommodate any individual or tenured performers from the theater company. When he got to the audition process, he faced many challenges. The play needed 76 people to form two casts because they were doing 22 performances—11 for each cast. Although this was a volunteer organization, 100 people came out and auditioned for Steve during 12 audition sessions. Steve wanted the process to be fair and respectful and to ensure an equal opportunity for everyone. Each person, regardless of age, experience, tenure, or political connections, had to audition. This included the old well-knowns who thought they were shoo-ins for a role, as well as Steve's supporters who thought their personal connection to him would guarantee them a role. But not everyone made it. Some people had to be cut, which was hard to do. Even in this phase, Steve approached the work as a learning opportunity for himself and for those who participated.

For final casting, Steve called the people who did not get a role in the play. He didn't have to do this, but he wanted to acknowledge their effort and contribution. There were tears, shock, and silences. He met with each person individually and gave them feedback. He acknowledged the hard work they did to prepare for and participate in the audition process. He also wanted them to know that although this play did not have a role for them, there could be other opportunities down the road that might be more suitable for them. He did not want to negatively affect their love of theater or discourage them from auditioning for other plays in the future.

Steve didn't like this part of the job, but it was necessary. He believed that the way he managed this process was just as important as the outcome. He also believed he needed to be accountable for his decisions and not cave in or shirk his responsibilities, which he said was a humbling experience. He knew he had his own personal development challenges while at the same time needed to coach and teach the cast and other people he had to work with. He recalled a time when he wasn't getting through to a young 11-year-old actor who had two left feet and was struggling onstage. He paired the 11-year-old with a 50-year-old to work together, which worked amazingly well. The child grew and then he flew! In this example, Steve used the community to teach each other. It was a perfect demonstration of the value of a mentoring partnership.

Steve viewed the theater as a family, and as such, he had to manage the group dynamics. During crunch time, there was a lot of conflict. To deal with it, he put in place a question-to-question process during the dry runs that required every actor, lighting person, and crew member to attend. This process cut through the interpersonal conflicts and helped everyone appreciate each other's talents and challenges. As a team, they learned to resolve sticky issues so they could "get on with the show."

Steve had to manage many volunteers. As he put it, they all had different needs, so he had to deal with each person differently to keep them motivated and engaged to keep volunteering. He could not afford to lose anyone. He also coached people who wanted coaching, and worked with others who needed coaching but may not have wanted it.

Steve even wrote a theme song that created a great team spirit. He also did little things like bringing drinks and treats to the rehearsals. These symbolic gestures meant a lot to the volunteer cast and crew members and helped them build relationships and ultimately strong bonds within their team.

As soon as the team bought into the vision, the play took on a life of its own. It was funded by the government and through some external donations from the public. The production went on to sell $70,000 in tickets and became the biggest-selling show for that community theater. Over 3,000 people of all ages attended. The play exceeded past attendance records at some of the more commercial shows. It was electrifying and generated buzz, and it was a big moment for the cast, theater, and community.

When asked about his reflections on his Use-of-Self as the director, Steve said he believed strongly in the power of teamwork. Without it, they would not have achieved the results that they achieved working together. Though he was only partly familiar with the LMC Framework and Process, he felt that he had applied them in this endeavor.

Steve believes the mandatory team meetings kept the vision alive. Everyone came away from team meetings feeling informed, involved, and educated about their own and each other's roles, contributions, challenges, interdependencies, and impact on the success of the play. Steve feels the way he led and managed the team using the guiding principles also helped them reach a quality of performance and a level of business success that they never would have previously imagined. He believes the facilitated discussions, direction, and way he helped with troubleshooting and problem solving made a significant impact. People trusted him, embraced the plan, were engaged, and had fun. If you recall, these are some of the characteristics of a cohesive team.

Throughout the journey, Steve had to be mindful of his intentions and the choices he made in his Use-of-Self. He asked himself, "Why am I making these choices? What are my preconceived notions about being a director? What impact do my preconceived notions have on my thinking and actions? What is helping me notice that I do have choices? Do I recognize that I do have choices, and that the choices I make can be transformative?"

Over the five months of working together on this production, Steve formed a theater family that grew together and made a huge impact in the lives of the performers, their families, and ultimately the entire community.

→ Maximizing the Power of the Team

The LMC Framework and Process and the teamwork tool and techniques can be customized and applied to any size or type of organization. As you can see through the content and examples in this chapter, developing teams to lead meaningful change is not achieved in the short term with a magic wand. It is an iterative process that continues throughout the lifecycle of the team and requires strong commitment and vision on the part of leaders, along with many activities and interventions that attend to the health and well-being of the team, the needs of each team member, and their interpersonal and group dynamics as people work together.

Large-scale transformational change work is complex. Often, the more complex the change, the greater the need for an expert design team to design, facilitate, coach, support, and evaluate the individual and team development process. If you work in a smaller organization, your leadership team may take on this role, or possibly include other internal or external people who have expertise and supports that you don't have within your organization.

Ultimately, creating cohesive teams and maximizing their power is an art, a craft, and a science. Teams are the glue that bonds people together for a shared purpose and engages their hearts, minds, and souls. With effective teamwork, collaboration, and partnerships, we can create workplaces where people thrive, find purpose, and achieve meaningful results that exceed expectations.

Chapter 7

←———————→

Case Study:

City of Ottawa—One City, One Team

As the new city manager at the City of Ottawa, Steve Kanellakos was tasked with improving the delivery of city services and creating long-term sustainability throughout the corporation. Based on his previous experience and tenure with the city, he knew that he needed a plan to transition to his new role and build a cohesive senior leadership team (SLT). Together they would develop a strategy to lead this meaningful change that would go beyond tactics to capture the hearts and souls of the people they led, worked with, and served.

This chapter is a case study about the SLT's journey through the first two years (2016 to 2018) of leading a transition and culture shift to adopt the mindset, values, and behaviors of "Servant Leadership" as the new guide to their day-to-day work.[22] It provides the background and context for this change, a summary of their approach through the lens of the LMC Process, and an overview of how they created a cohesive team that inspired people across the corporation to embrace the shared purpose "One City, One Team" to achieve results that were far greater than any single contribution.[23]

→ **Background to the Case**

Ottawa is Canada's capital and the fourth-largest city in Canada, comparable in size with cities such as Austin, Jacksonville, San Francisco, and San Jose in the United States. It has approximately 17,000 municipal workers serving 1 million residents. In the beginning of this journey, the city was operating as a federation, a hierarchical organization where services were siloed and not working toward a common purpose.

In addition to needing to maintain regular operations and delivering city services, the city was facing a significant year in 2017 as it prepared to host year-long celebrations for Canada's 150th anniversary, including Canada Day festivities that would be held over four days, with expected crowds of 750,000 people from across the country and beyond streaming into the downtown core of the city in July. At this same time, the city still needed to work on its infrastructure and a project to build a new light-rail system.

It was in this context that Steve stepped into the role of city manager. Immediately, during the first few days of taking on his new role, he also had to deal with a major emergency situation that would pull all the city leaders, including the mayor, together to respond. A large water main broke and created a giant sinkhole next to a major shopping center in a downtown mall, collapsing a street and causing a gas leak, which forced the evacuation of all nearby businesses. The water leak was also near the construction site of the new light-rail system, which included a tunnel and stations being dug beneath the downtown core. Fortunately, no one was hurt.

This sinkhole emergency triggered an urgent call to work as a unified organization to fix the problem. It became clear that everyone had to change mindsets to keep the city safe and make it a great place to live, work, and play in the short and long terms. Throughout the course of the next two years, the city would face additional emergencies, including a long-term care crisis, two floods, two tornado events, and a bus crash that resulted in multiple deaths and significant injuries.

→ Leadership, Alignment, Teamwork, and Collaboration Plan

Steve and the senior leadership team led and managed the transition process and culture shift to acting as "One City, One Team" through two years of substantial change and crisis management. In the context of the LMC Process, Figure 9 summarizes their work in each of the four stages, while Table 8 shows a Master Change Plan that outlines how Steve and the SLT planned the first eight months of activities. Look these over to become familiar with their high-level view and then follow me as we walk through the four stages in detail in the rest of the chapter.

→ Stage 1: Alignment

Goals: Create overall transition strategy for One City, One Team; establish Servant Leadership values and behaviors; assess priorities

Steve began by appointing a director to lead the transition and form a small transition team to help him plan, develop, and implement the first 30 days of his transition to city manager. This team quickly expanded to include additional experts to help them design a new organizational structure, choose a new senior leadership team, develop the transition plans for each department of city services, and ensure their alignment with each other and with the entire corporation.

During this time, I worked alongside the director and the transition team as an external organizational development and change consultant. I provided coaching, helped develop and evaluate the transition plans, and created tools and a process for the SLT development program.

As next steps, Steve conducted wide-ranging consultations to deepen his understanding of the need for change and

Figure 9 **City of Ottawa's Transformation Summarized in the LMC Process**

KEY ELEMENTS

- One City, One Team
- Servant Leadership
- Consultation processes
- Alignment of strategy: city and council priorities, structure, budget, people, and culture
- Transition task team
- Transition plans
- Organizational structure and governance

KEY ELEMENTS

- SLT development program with three working sessions: Alignment, Priority Setting, and Change Leadership
- *Leading Transitions Handbook*
- Leading Transitions Self-Development Guide
- Coaching
- Cross-department, city-wide collaboration and teamwork

KEY ELEMENTS

- Transition task team coaching, facilitation, and support
- Implementation of the transition plans and process across the city and within each department
- SLT interview
- Implementation of SLT and individual development plans
- Three SLT online surveys
- Pulse checks with staff, clients, political stakeholders, and partners

KEY ELEMENTS

- Checkpoint evaluation of achievements and impacts on people, culture, business results, budget, and priorities
- Reflections on leading meaningful change
- SLT interviews
- SLT online survey
- Develop priorities for SLT and next steps to sustain and refresh the plan

◄──── Continuous cycles of evaluation to measure results and impacts ────►

Table 8 City of Ottawa Master Change Plan for the First Eight Months

Where Do You Expect to Be in the Change Process?		
Understand Months 1 to 2	**Align** Months 3 to 4	**Plan and Execute** Months 5 to 8
Corporate Activities and Key Milestones		
• Council consultation process	• Council endorsement of organizational design and governance structure	• Council update on the transition plan and endorsement of the go-forward strategy, priorities, and budget
Organizational Alignment		
• Assess current state and priorities • Conduct SLT consultation process • Develop workplan • Assess organizational design, including capacity, priorities, principles, model, and accountability-governance framework • Conduct impact analysis • Develop people plan and change strategy	• Develop SLT transition strategy • SLT lead alignment processes in their departments • Develop new department organizational structures • Develop business support model, business transformation plan, and departmental transition plans • Conduct general manager consultation process to obtain feedback and input • Develop opportunities list and recommendations for council • Align organizational priorities with the budget	• Implement transition plans • Conduct consultation process • Finalize general manager alignment process and priorities with budget process • Prepare final report on the way forward and recommendations to council

Supports		
• Form transition task team, processes, and tools to support people through the transition and transformation	• Conduct SLT working session 1: Alignment • Conduct general manager interviews and needs assessment • Develop SLT transition strategy • Coach and facilitate peer learning	• Conduct SLT working session 2: Priority Setting • Conduct SLT working session 3: Change Leadership (shared vision of the way forward, defined mandate for extended management teams, and decision-making processes) • Implement SLT personal leadership transition plans
Communications and Engagement		
• Develop and implement the transition and communications plan for the city manager's first 60 days • Conduct employee engagement sessions that include all employee levels	• Develop a report on employee engagement sessions • Develop transition plan and organizational alignment toolkit and supports • Develop transition and communications plan, products, and supports for alignment and planning	• Implement communications strategy • Conduct employee engagement sessions (managers and all staff)

to develop the guiding principles and priorities. In the first 60 days, he consulted with the mayor and city council, their staffs, and important city stakeholders. He also reached out to over 3,200 city employees through direct engagement sessions with groups at various sites. During this time, he received close to 15,200 ideas on what to consider when building the transition plan for the entire organization.

The consultation process helped Steve read the pulse of the organization and deepened his understanding of the problems and the areas that needed improvement. An overwhelming number of respondents (71 percent) to surveys he conducted stated that the organization's overall effectiveness had to be addressed. The top concerns were flattening the leadership hierarchy, cutting bureaucracy, supporting staff to do their jobs, and planning for leadership succession. Improving front-line service delivery was also a key consideration to align the change effort with the city's overall transition plan. After meeting with the city council and their staff, he also concluded that he needed to create a new organizational structure that met the council's priorities and increased the organization's effectiveness, yet did not disrupt city services.

Steve's consultation process allowed him to create a plan for the next six months that would guide him and the new SLT through the transition. The gamut of changes would require numerous culture shifts to meet the short-term needs of the city and position it for long-term success. Table 9 synthesizes the various culture shifts that Steve and the SLT realized they needed to strive for.

By the end of the first 60 days, the city council endorsed the SLT's new vision, which they named "One City, One Team." They also approved the next phase of the transition plan, focused on seven priorities that crossed all departments:

1. Financial sustainability
2. City building

Table 9 City of Ottawa Culture Shift Requirements

Transition From	Transition To
Silos and competition	One City, One Team
Hierarchical and bureaucratic chain of command; accountability and decision making at the top	Flatter organization; decisions made at the right level; clear accountabilities and responsibilities at all levels
SLT • Too large • Blend of expertise that made it difficult to focus on strategic issues • Bottleneck for problem solving and timely and accurate decision making	SLT • Smaller size to facilitate teamwork, collaboration, problem solving, and decision making • Members with long service, broad reach of expertise, and a common history with the city • Agenda focused on the strategic direction and open discussion
Leadership style: direct or jump to action	Leadership style: collaborate, develop, coach, mentor, and delegate; shared values and commitment to Servant Leadership behaviors
Constant churn of priorities	Focused priorities
Disengaged workforce	Engaged and empowered workforce
Risk-averse	Risk-taking
No succession plan	Succession plan and career development
Dissatisfied citizens	Satisfied citizens

3. Social infrastructure
4. Building a light-rail system and putting it into service
5. Service delivery
6. Organizational effectiveness
7. Celebrating Canada's 150th anniversary

They also put in place a new organizational structure with consolidated departments and a smaller, more streamlined, and more empowered SLT composed of nine general managers, reduced from 21 senior leaders on the previous SLT. By consolidating departments, the administration could work more effectively to meet the council's priorities and better serve the public. The new structure was designed to

- establish a leadership team committed to deliver a budget limited to a 2 percent tax increase;
- provide a clear focus for all staff in support of the city's priorities;
- flatten levels of senior management and simplify reporting relationships with clear lines of accountability;
- improve peer-to-peer relationships and empower and engage management and staff to make decisions;
- break down silos to promote greater collaboration across services and departments;
- streamline business processes to maximize value to customers and citizens; and, with an eye to the future,
- enable better succession planning and career development at all levels of the organization.

→ Stage 2: Integration

Goals: Develop and implement SLT development program, Leading Transitions Handbook, *and Leading Transitions Self-Development Guide*

The focus of this stage was on ongoing leadership development and ensuring the overall alignment of organizational priorities as the process moved into stage 3. The rationale was that SLT was a new and unique team, although most members (including me) already had a long history and deep roots working in the city. SLT members enjoyed high credibility and good working relationships with people inside the corporation and in the community. Their shared history and experience with the organization helped the team quickly adopt and model the culture of One City, One Team and the Servant Leadership values and behaviors. Another characteristic that members shared was that all of them were eligible for retirement within one to four years, which put the spotlight on the need for succession planning across the city, but which also created an opportunity for each member to reflect on the legacy they wanted to leave behind, both personally and professionally.

However, despite this common ground, the team was still new at working together as a smaller SLT. They needed to identify and understand the problems across the city and build solid plans to address them. Leading the city's transformation was the first task they would work on together. It was a high-profile change, and priority setting and change leadership were vitally important. The SLT members were full of hope that they could do it, yet they knew it would not be an easy journey. The change was loaded with political expectations and complex challenges that they would need to overcome together.

To support them through their own transition to their new roles and as they did their work, the plan called for the SLT to participate in a multifaceted development program called the Leading Transitions Program. This was implemented over the next six months so that it would overlap with the actual work that would be done during stage 3: action. The program included three full-day working sessions, plus intersession activities. These activities were customized to

- develop a strategy to lead and implement the city's transition plan;
- create a shared understanding of the transition plan and the way forward;
- create a shared understanding and a common vision of their roles and responsibilities and how they would work together as one team;
- obtain tools and supports they needed to develop and advance their departmental transition plans;
- obtain supports for their personal leadership development plan;
- deepen their understanding of the need for change, the strategic priorities, and the principles that would shape the new organizational design and governance framework;
- obtain clarity on their mission and role as a member of the SLT and as general manager of their department;
- obtain their input on the transition plan and deliverables; and
- obtain their commitment for the way forward.

An evaluation process was used throughout the program to assess its design and content, the SLT members' learning and development experience, and their reflections on leading and managing the transition. This evaluation also helped identify running themes and emerging patterns that needed to be addressed to support the culture shifts.

Table 10 shows the elements of the SLT Leading Transitions Program. This table is effectively an expanded view of the supports row of the Master Change Plan shown in Table 8.

Let's examine the goals and events of each of the working sessions to understand how the process supported the city's change effort.

Table 10 City of Ottawa SLT Leading Transitions Program

Alignment Process		
SLT WS1: Alignment	SLT WS2: Priority Setting	SLT WS3: Change Leadership
Intersession Activities		
<ul><li>Obtain coaching and support from transition team.</li><li>Implement working sessions and cross-department collaboration activities.</li><li>Develop and implement departmental transition plans aligning strategy, structure, budget, people, and culture.</li><li>Develop and implement general manager and SLT development plans.</li></ul>		
Evaluating Culture Shifts Process		
<ul><li>SLT individual interview 1</li><li>SLT evaluation survey 1</li></ul>	<ul><li>SLT evaluation survey 2</li></ul>	<ul><li>SLT evaluation survey 3</li></ul>

SLT Working Session 1: Alignment

The first session reviewed and discussed the five key themes uncovered during Steve's consultation process—leadership, alignment, teamwork, collaboration, and focused results—grounding them in real-life examples that team members could relate to. These themes would become the principles that the SLT would use to guide their work throughout the process.

In the first session, each SLT member was given a *Leading Transitions Handbook* to help them develop their departmental transition plans and align them with the city's larger transition plan. It included timelines, tools, supports, and resources. Each member of the new SLT was asked to design their own departmental transition plans to mirror the larger corporate organizational structure and principles created in stage 1 to update the city's operating model. This was a complex process, and many SLT members had to make difficult decisions involving their staff, budget, and the impact of their departmental transition plans on the services they provided to city residents. By the end of the first meeting, the SLT members signed a call to action that included the following tasks:

- Develop a transition plan for their department.

- Align their departmental transition plan with the city's business transformation plan.

- Understand and create the support for the new organizational design and accountability framework.

- Clarify the direction going forward, accept the new priorities, and affirm their role in leading and managing the next phase of the transformation.

- Identify impacts, concerns, and issues that needed to be addressed in the next 30 to 90 days and how those would affect the entire city.

- Develop a people plan that included leadership development, succession planning, and needed supports to lead and manage their people throughout the transition process.

- Develop a communications plan that included key messages and a consultation process to help them lead and manage the implementation of the organizational alignment process and transition plan in their departments and with their stakeholders.

- Create a consultation process to obtain feedback and input from their staff and stakeholders.

SLT members also received a Leading Transitions Self-Development Guide to reflect on their own new roles as general managers and members of the SLT (a generic version, the Leading Meaningful Change Self-Development Guide, is included in the part 2 toolkit). They used this guide to develop their personal transition plan, which they would share with Steve for his input and feedback. The themes and patterns from this exercise also informed the corporate learning and development strategy that was developed later in the process. The transition team assisted the SLT members as they developed and implemented their transition plans and the intersession activities.

SLT Working Session 2: Priority Setting

This working session occurred several months after the first working session, so SLT members were already engaged in developing their departmental transition plans. As prework for this session, SLT members had to work with their transition team advisor to prepare a presentation on their transition plans that they would share in the working session. The transition teams also met prior to the session to review all the transition plans and track the themes and patterns. From that, they prepared a summary report that they sent to the SLT members for their review prior to the session. This process helped develop a common understanding among all SLT members and the transition team about the current status of the departments, the common issues and concerns that crossed over all service areas, and the unique department-specific issues. This exercise was invaluable in assessing the alignment between the overall city-wide strategy and priorities and the individual transition and departmental plans. It revealed the synergies, dependencies, interdependencies, and opportunities for collaboration that would be discussed in the working session.

- As part of this process, SLT members also participated in individual interviews with me in my role as a coach

to the team. Together, we began crafting their personal
leadership development plans.

- In the full-day working session, our objectives were to
- create an opportunity for all SLT members to learn more
  about each other as leaders and how they saw their role
  on the SLT;
- provide an opportunity to discuss each person's
  reflections on leading through the transition; and
- create a common understanding of the themes and
  patterns, both current and emerging, as they led the
  transition.

SLT Working Session 3: Change Leadership

By this working session, SLT members were nearly six
months into their transition work. In this full-day session,
they reviewed the results of the second evaluation survey
and discussed their progress on implementing their transition plans and culture shifts. They completed a customized version of the Evaluating and Sustaining Meaningful
Change Exercise described in part 2 in order to assess their
progress on their own transition plans and culture shifts.
They also finalized an SLT charter, mandate, and governance
process. Lastly, they planned next steps for their personal
development as general managers and how they would sustain the cohesiveness of the SLT going forward.

All three working sessions also featured a communications exercise designed to help the SLT develop key messages about the transition plan and next steps for each of
the audiences and stakeholders. This exercise helped the
team practice their communication skills, speak with one
voice, and ensure consistent messaging across the city.

→ Stage 3: Action

Goals: Champion leadership, teamwork, and collaboration

This stage involved applying the tools, putting the transition plan into action, and monitoring and measuring the

planned and emergent impacts. (To be clear, segments of stage 2 and stage 3 overlapped, in that the second and third working sessions discussed above occurred during milestone periods in stage 3.)

To start their action plan, each SLT member used the same consultation approach as Steve to learn about the priorities in their own departments. In a coordinated and parallel process, each general manager, along with their respective management teams and other people in their department, designed their own departmental transition plan, ensuring that it aligned with the overall corporate transition plan and adhered to the organizational design principles. At this level of the organizational design, the following key changes were implemented:

- Departments were flattened, with fewer management levels and increased accountability.
- Business support services and functions were streamlined into consistent branches across the organization.
- Service delivery functions that had been integrated into different departments were consolidated.
- This new structure promoted greater efficiencies, identified clear accountabilities, empowered employees, and helped create succession plans that would ensure long-term sustainability and quality service delivery throughout the city.

This transition was a complex process and had to consider the entire organizational system. SLT members also had to focus on their personal transitions as they took on their new roles while at the same time leading others through the transformation process in their departments across the city, including community partners and other stakeholders. Change thus had to happen at the individual, SLT, organization, and community levels. The working sessions of stage 2 supported people through these challenges.

Strengthening the Transition Team

By this stage, the changes were more complex and needed to involve more people across the corporation, so the transition team was expanded to include additional expertise and supports. The new service innovation and performance department (SIPD) was created, led by its own general manager, and a new business integration team (BIT), comprising business support services (BSS) managers from each department, was formed to play an active role in executing the transition plans. This team worked as internal consultants, advisors, and coaches to the SLT members and to their extended departmental teams and other project teams across the city. BSS managers provided expertise in strategy development, change leadership and change management, organizational development, governance, human resources, organizational design and effectiveness, finance, information technology, and communications.

Table 11 summarizes the responsibilities of the SLT general managers and the SIPD and the BIT, illustrating how they all worked together as partners to lead and manage the transition.

→ Stage 4: Renewal

Goals: Conduct evaluation process; understand and evaluate culture shifts

The change process and culture shifts were evaluated throughout the transition process. The major evaluations that took place during stages 1 through 3 included three SLT online surveys and a set of SLT individual interviews. The SLT also conducted several pulse surveys with staff, stakeholders, city councillors, and community partners. The final evaluation, done as part of my research during the renewal stage, included a second set of SLT interviews and a fourth online survey. Let's look at the intermediary online and phone interview evaluations before discussing the final evaluation.

Table 11 **Summary of Responsibilities for Leading and Managing the Transition at the City of Ottawa**

SLT General Manager Responsibilities	SIPD and BIT Responsibilities for Supporting SLT
• Champion, steward, and lead the development and implementation of the city's transformation strategy and transition plans in their departments • Align their departmental plans with One City, One Team; Servant Leadership values and behaviors; and the city's priorities, budget, timelines, and people plan • Participate in three SLT working sessions • Develop key messages, provide content, and communicate regularly to Steve and each other on the progress on the plan	• Lead and manage the development and implementation of the city's transition plan and alignment process, including people, organizational culture, and communications strategies • Provide expertise in human resources, organizational development, change, process improvement, performance analytics, communications, administration, and program management • Provide dedicated resources, a framework, a process, and tools to develop and evaluate the department alignment process, transition plans, and organizational culture • Design and facilitate the formation of the SLT mandate, governance structure, and working sessions • Oversee the design and management of the organizational assessment and the development of the departmental organizational structure to ensure cross-departmental integration

Online Surveys

The first three SLT online surveys were completed after each SLT working session. These online surveys helped assess the

- progress made up to that point on advancing the transition plan, objectives, and results;
- effectiveness of the program design, tools, and supports;
- development of change leadership competencies; and
- adoption of the new values and servant leader behaviors.

These surveys included several self-assessments that we tracked over time and reviewed at the start of each working session. The results of each survey were rolled up into a team report to help the SLT develop a collective understanding of their personal and team journey, celebrate their successes, and make faster course corrections as needed. Here are some of the survey questions:

Change Leadership Competencies. Each SLT member was asked to answer each question using a scale from 1 = no agreement to 8 = full agreement.

1. I understand the vision, direction, and context for leading the changes.
2. I have strategies in place to lead the transition in my department.
3. I have strategies in place to lead the transition with key stakeholders outside my department.
4. I am confident in my ability to lead the transition at the city.
5. I understand my role in leading the changes.
6. I am effective developing and implementing strategies to help people overcome resistance and adapt to the changes.
7. I am effective working in the SLT to lead change.

8. I am effective working with my management team to lead change.
9. I am effective building collaborative relationships to lead and implement the transition plan.
10. I am effective communicating change.
11. I am effective engaging my staff in the change process.
12. I am effective developing, coaching, and mentoring others.
13. I am achieving my goals and objectives in leading this transition.
14. I have effective practices, tools, and support for my own learning and development.
15. I am fully engaged in this process.

Values Self-Assessment. In each online survey, SLT members were asked to respond to the question: How well am I living our SLT values and behaviors?

1. Trust
2. Respect
3. Collaboration
4. Teamwork: One Team, One Voice
5. Integrity
6. Communication

Servant Leadership Self-Assessment. Each SLT member was asked to respond to this question: How well am I living our Servant Leadership competencies? [24]

1. *Person of character:* I make insightful, ethical, and principle-centered decisions; I am able to maintain integrity; I demonstrate humility; I serve a Higher Purpose.

2. *Puts people first:* I am able to help others meet their highest priority development needs; I display a servant's heart; I mentor and develop others; I show care and concern.

3. *Skilled communicator:* I listen earnestly and speak effectively; I demonstrate empathy; I invite feedback; I communicate persuasively.

4. *Compassionate collaborator:* I am able to strengthen relationships, support diversity, and create a sense of belonging; I express appreciation; I build teams; I collaborate and create communities; I negotiate conflict.

5. *Has foresight:* I imagine possibilities, anticipate the future, and proceed with clarity of purpose; I am a visionary; I display creativity and innovation; I take courageous and decisive action.

6. *Systems thinker:* I think and act strategically, lead change effectively, and balance the whole with the sum of its parts; I am comfortable with complexity; I demonstrate adaptability and agility; I consider the "Greater Good."

7. *Leads with moral authority:* I am worthy of respect, inspire trust and confidence, and establish equality standards for performance; I accept and delegate responsibility; I share power and control; I empower others; I create a culture of accountability.

The data from the online evaluation process were invaluable in helping us validate the success of the transition plan process and the SLT's development in the moment and over time, as well as identify themes and patterns that still needed to be addressed to shift the corporate culture and support the departmental transition plans. The results were shared with SLT members to help them reflect on their journey and plan next steps for their own leadership development. For example, in the first working session at the end of 2017, SLT members identified the following measures of success as they looked forward to 2018. This is what they hoped to achieve and actually realized:

1. We are living our values and culture of One City, One Team. General managers, departments, and city council are aligned.

2. The new organizational structure is effective. We have in place a strong leadership team and highly functioning cohesive department teams. People understand their roles, responsibilities, and accountabilities. SLT meetings are effective and supported by the city manager's office.

3. The work climate is positive. People understand how they contribute and have a sense of fulfillment, meaning, and satisfaction with their work and life. Employee engagement survey scores have improved.

4. I have achieved my personal development plan and transition goals. I am still engaged, proud of my legacy, making a difference, and contributing to a higher purpose.

5. We have demonstrated improvements in service. Citizen satisfaction scores have improved and there is a reduction in complaints. Council and partner feedback is positive.

6. A talent management and succession plan is in place and working well.

7. We have financial stability.

8. Light-rail transit is in revenue service. (This goal was still a work in progress at the time of this publication.)

In addition, by the end of the first and second stages of the change process, there was a 4 percent increase in employee job satisfaction, and the city had achieved the corporate efficiency target of $14 million for both 2017 and 2018 through a combination of efficiencies, new revenues, and alignments. These included

- increased revenues through property sales;
- implementation of the new senior leadership structure;
- completion of an organizational alignment process;
- implementation of the departmental transition plans;
- completion of a service review program, including a review of winter operations; and
- completion of an administrative restructuring.

Phone Interviews

SLT members also participated in two 60-minute phone interviews. The first one was to serve as a baseline and was conducted at the beginning of stage 1. These interviews were designed to help SLT members reflect on their personal transition and identify their needs for further personal development as they moved into their new role as general manager and as they managed their departmental transition plans. The phone interview was also an opportunity for coaching and supporting their personal leadership development. Through this process, their feedback was used to inform the design of the overall leadership development strategy and specifically the Leading Transitions Program discussed above.

Each SLT member was asked the following questions during the interview:

1. What must we keep top of mind as we design a leadership development strategy to support you as you transition into your new role and lead the development and implementation of the city's transition plan?

2. As part of the Leading Transitions Program, we will be conducting three working sessions for the SLT. What approaches and topics must we include in our design that will support your learning and advance your work?

3. As general manager and given your new mandate, what are your goals and aspirations for the next 90 days?

4. What supports and development do you and your management team need to be successful working with your stakeholders?

5. What personal, departmental, and organizational effectiveness goals do you want to reach by the end of this term of council?

6. How will you measure success at the end of this term of council?

7. What do we need to ensure your full participation in the upcoming working sessions?

8. Do you have any additional suggestions or comments?

Final Evaluation

In this case study, the final evaluation of the alignment and transition process consisted of a second set of SLT interviews and a fourth SLT online survey. This evaluation process was completed in December 2018, which was a significant milestone. It was the end of the city council's term and just as the new council was formed. The results of this evaluation process helped the SLT to reflect on their journey and plan their next steps.

The second set of SLT interviews and the results of the SLT online survey were consistent with those conducted earlier and discussed above. The survey revealed a positive trend in meeting and exceeding expectations in leading the various departmental transitions and in the overall meaningful change journey. SLT members expressed some uncertainty about the future work they still needed to do as the SLT and in their role as general managers to address the anticipated changes coming from a newly elected provincial government and expectations of a newly elected city council.

This was also a time of renewal for the SLT. They were transitioning to working with the new council and needed to refresh or adapt their plan for the next four years to ensure it was aligned with the new council's commitments. They were reflecting on what they needed to do to sustain the changes, the culture of One City, One Team, and the Servant Leadership values and behaviors. It was also a time to reenergize and renew their commitment as the SLT responsible for leading the next phase of the city's transformational journey.

Given this context, there was general agreement among all SLT members about the focus for their next steps:

- Sustaining cohesive teamwork in the SLT
- Continuing to build a culture of One City, One Team
- Continuing to model and live the Servant Leadership values and behaviors
- Developing supervisors and front-line staff
- Continuing with succession planning
- Focusing on realizing results, outcomes, and the return on investment

As you can see, this SLT went through a significant journey. They embodied a shared purpose and established a solid foundation for One City, One Team and the Servant Leadership values and behaviors that are sure to be sustained in the next phases of change in Ottawa. They were also very successful working with teams and teams of teams and collaborating across the city. For some, their journey continues, and for others, their legacy was just beginning as they approached retirement.

→ Reflections on the Journey Two Years Later

As part of my research for this book, I met with the SLT members two years after the start of our work together to gather their reflections about leading a meaningful change (one member had already retired and been replaced with a new team member). This group interview took place one year after my last working session with them. They had already participated in the fourth SLT online survey and the second individual interview with me. Their personal memories and experiences are worth citing, as they demonstrate the power of the team and how to create and lead truly meaningful change.

First and foremost, all members of the SLT were honest, humble, and sincere as they participated in this reflection process. They were proud of how they had worked together to foster a culture of One City, One Team and modeled the Servant Leadership values and behaviors for their departments. They shared a deep appreciation for having had the opportunity to work together as a team and were very proud of the work they accomplished and the contributions they made, and continue to make today, to ensure they leave the city a better place. They affirmed that they had each other's back in good times and especially when they were under fire, which is when it counts. They learned a lot over those first two years and are still learning about leading change today. They valued and appreciated working together to develop their strategies and solve problems. They had high trust and respect for each other. They established a strong foundation, ethical decision-making processes, integrated planning, and a city culture that staff and residents feel proud of.

The SLT was confident that the culture of One City, One Team and the Servant Leadership values and behaviors that permeate across the city could be sustained over time. When reflecting on their work on the SLT and with their teams, partners, stakeholders, and city council, many talked about achieving a truly *shared* purpose. They used the pronoun "we"; no one used "I." This speaks volumes about their shared values that they continue to model and hold each other to account for. All SLT members also spoke about the strong leadership and coaching they received from city manager Steve Kanellakos, whom they saw as a key contributor to their success.

Reflecting back over the two years since my work with them, it was striking that no one said that they had a defining moment when they regretted taking on their new job and wanted to leave. People definitely faced serious challenges, such as dealing with the sinkhole, floods, tornados, a long-term care crisis, development of the light-rail transit system, and other public and political challenges—all while maintaining daily operations and delivering the usual services. Despite these pressures, during each crisis, each general manager looked deep inside and asked themselves, "If not me, then who?" In response, they each stepped up to lead the way.

In the surveys and interviews at the end of the process, I captured a number of conclusions that individuals drew about meaningful change. These are some of their thoughts, supported by direct comments from various SLT members:

1. *Meaningful change is a personal feeling of accomplishment.* Steve phrased this conclusion the best when he said, "When you are successful leading meaningful change, it means that you have captured the hearts and souls of the people. They believe in a higher purpose, something greater than their own single contribution."

Others described meaningful change as "the magic sauce." "There is something happening. I can feel it. Things are changing. It's hard to put into words and measure it."

2. *Leading meaningful change must have a realistic plan that has meaning for people.*
Meaningful change is more than designing and implementing a new process, policy, or procedure. The vision, destination, and method for how you will get there must be legitimate, realistic, and compelling for people to want to achieve it. They need mutual awareness (not only one perspective) and understanding of the desires, needs, and challenges of the clients, stakeholders, staff, partners, or anyone involved or impacted by the changes.

One general manager described it this way: "Meaningful change means that people find value and meaning in the change. The change is thoughtful, relevant, and results in actions that help people behave differently, adopt new behaviors, and achieve the desired results." In this case, the general manager was proud of how they had built teams working across the city, specifically with the SLT and their departmental leadership teams working with the extended departmental leadership team, which included all directors from across the city. She was also proud of how they had put into place the teams that provided business supports such as human resources, organizational development, information technology, communications, and other services across the city. They persevered through many new challenges and delivered services that added value, as explained by one general manager who used the business support services. She described one defining moment of "collective brilliance":

> This moment of collective brilliance occurred in the early part of the transition. SLT had participated in a very long strategic planning session. At the end of the all-day working session, the wall was full of divergent ideas and priorities posted on sticky notes. I remember being overwhelmed and thinking the plan would be impossible to achieve given our workload and capacity. Two or three days later, the service innovation and performance department (SIPD) who designed and facilitated the process pulled together the results of the session on one page that included three key areas of priority: our people, our service, and our city. This was a moment of collective brilliance. SLT could not have done this work without the SIPD team. It was an epiphany and concrete example of how we as the SLT would continue to work together with the SIPD. At this moment of the presentation, all the "noise" fell away. There were no more "me" issues. No more "the sky is falling" comments;

instead, anything was possible. Everyone was on board, including councillors, partners, and staff.

3. *Leading meaningful change must consider the well-being of the people involved and impacted.*

Leading meaningful change must consider not only the work that needs to be done, but also how you lead people through the changes. You especially need to focus on the well-being of the people in the approach you take to develop the plan, assess the impacts, and create the organization required for long-term success. This means developing people so they can be the best they can be to serve others, including clients, residents, stakeholders, and each other.

In Ottawa, the SLT built a solid foundation for fostering a culture of One City, One Team by making the development of people a priority. They talked about how to eliminate barriers and took action. They asked themselves, "What's working and why? What's not working and why not?" at all levels of the organization. Accountability was no longer just a template; they were living it in their day-to-day actions. They put in place training and development supports, including leadership forums, formal leadership development programs, coaching and mentoring, and a fair and clear succession planning process. In addition, they put a lot of effort into communicating and engaging others across the corporation.

One general manager said, "Great leaders of people are always evolving as leaders themselves, and building their internal supports. People at the city are talking about 'how' they are developing their people and sharing their success stories and wise practices. There is a positive energy and buzz that is exciting and palpable."

Another general manager spent time understanding the employees by focusing on their needs as people, not just on the role they played and the work that had to be done. She learned about their career aspirations and interests, as well as their desired impact and legacy. She aligned the development plan with the vision of One City, One Team and the principles and values of Servant Leadership, then put in place the processes, tools, and supports to develop people in real time.

4. *Meaningful change requires leadership.*
SLT members believe they played a key role in leading the culture shifts by modeling the values and behaviors of One City, One Team and Servant Leadership in everything they said and did inside and outside the organization. SLT members were committed to creating opportunities to grow their people and adopt a new mindset that would help each person be successful. They wanted and expected everyone to participate in the journey. They developed values and principles that shaped the way they coordinated and collaborated with each other in the SLT and with others in the city. They developed strong relationships, making it a priority to take the time to understand the people issues by walking around and checking the pulse of how people were thinking and feeling. They listened to find out what was working and not. They incorporated what they were learning in their plans. They kept at it and never stopped.

Leaders need to be present and in the moment to inspire, coach, mentor, and develop people to embrace the vision and see themselves as an integral part of the change. One general manager described it in the following way: "Leadership is about supporting the organization and our people so they are equipped to provide high-quality services that are relevant and responsive to the needs of the community, and at the same time, make the workplace better by making it easier to deliver services." Other leaders talked about leaving a legacy and ensuring that their work had a lasting, positive impact in the lives of others and made the city a better place.

5. *Leading meaningful change requires continuous evaluation.*
There must be continuous monitoring of how well we, as the

leadership team, and the organization are doing as we live and work with a shared purpose, mindset, values, and behaviors. Success happens when the desired changes occur as the natural way of working and when you as a leader don't have to manage them. It happens when people appreciate the value and meaning of the changes and can apply them in their day-to-day work.

6. *Leading meaningful change requires teamwork.*
Change can be easy to make in good and stable times, but it can be especially challenging when we are dealing with emergencies and are under fire. Although I conducted the phone interviews with individuals, it was striking that they consistently spoke with one voice, as one team. They said that they could pick up the phone and call anyone around the table for advice and help if and when needed. One general manager expressed this sentiment as follows: "I know my SLT colleagues have my back. I can reach out to anyone and they will say 'Okay, what do you need?' I know I can count on their support and make it happen."

→ The SLT's Advice for Other Teams
In my meeting with the SLT, I also asked if they had any advice for other teams who are leading a meaningful change journey. These are their recommendations:

1. *Spend time planning and aligning:* Don't underestimate the value of the alignment phase. Create a common purpose, values, and principles that will guide your work. Ensure your vision and strategy are aligned with your organization's priorities, operations, and business. Make sure you do this first, then focus on the people. Just look around and get out of your comfort zone. Purposely sit with other people whom you don't normally work with; this will result in a different conversation and learning experience for you and others.

2. *Develop a concrete, clear plan:* Be strategic, laser-focused, methodical, and tactical in planning your change. It's not enough to just say the words, "We are going to change." You need to figure out what you want and need. Be specific about what is changing and then constantly check for progress and understanding about what people need, where they are being successful or not, and the impacts of the change on the entire system. This will help people to see change happening and their role in the process, as well as their impact. What gets measured gets implemented.

3. *Model and embody the change:* Take time to develop change leadership skills—both individually and as a team.

4. *Engage others:* Make time for people. Sometimes you can't hurry them. Sometimes you have to take time to talk, listen, reassure, coach, and have meaningful conversations. Understand and address their "me" issues. Expect people to contribute and help them understand how they will be included and what their opportunities are to provide input. Engage and involve staff and those impacted in the process of understanding why the change is needed. As for the changes, seek out their thoughts and ideas every step of the process. Begin with "This is what I am thinking..." or "Here is what is happening...," then ask, "What do you think?" and "What do you want to accomplish?" Walk around and check the pulse regularly, and keep at it.

5. *Honor teamwork:* Pick the right team. Take time to form and develop a cohesive senior leadership team who will work together, have each other's backs, and support each other through good times and under fire, when it counts. Pay attention to the team's dynamics. It takes work, just like a good marriage.

6. *Create a shared legacy:* Make a commitment to each other. Keep your principles alive by living them. Respect each other. Trust yourself and trust others on the team. Develop ways to work with the diversity of opinions that will make the team stronger.

7. *Master your Use-of-Self:* Develop empathy. Be humble, be self-aware, and understand your impact. Leave your ego at the door. Remember everyone is on the same team. Be easy on yourself and remember that sometimes you don't get it right. Be yourself and be true to your style and personality. You are the real deal. Stretch yourself. Get out of your comfort zone and be vulnerable.

8. *Be open to feedback:* Be open to receiving feedback and constantly seek the feedback you need, not just feedback that will make you feel good. Pay attention to the intent of the message. Identify your go-to people to get meaningful feedback.

9. *Build support systems:* It is lonely at the top. Find ways to know how and when to rely on others. Pick strong allies at the beginning and be patient.

10. *Develop your people:* Grow your people. It's hard to do if you are just building a name for yourself. Focus not only on providing people with the tools, resources, and supports to lead and manage change, but also on seeking the change in mindset required to work differently. Model the values and behaviors that are needed and be clear on what is expected when people show up for work. This change in mindset and behavior is the real stuff. It's inside you.

11. *Pay attention to the financial realities and context of the changes:* However, don't let these stop you from driving change or advancing your strategic initiatives. You might be surprised with the results you can achieve when you are leading in the right place with the right people who have the right skills and clarity about the direction. Anything is possible!

12. *Build and nurture relationships and networks:* Develop the skills to work with and manage the political, stakeholder, and partner relationships and networks. This too requires building cohesive teamwork.

13. *Communicate:* Maintain open, honest communication. Share the employee engagement results and recommendations so people can contribute and develop solutions. Make sure you, as a leader, are present and visible with the people you are leading in operations. It is not always easy to do, given the many geographic locations and the daily pressures you may experience on the front line. Spend time doing ride-alongs and check-ins with people to learn about their day-to-day concerns. Let people walk you through their day and tell you what they are thinking as well as their issues and ideas for improvements.

This approach to leading meaningful change is more effective than the top-down hierarchical change paradigm. The LMC Framework and Process is a collaborative effort and personal journey. It is well worth it because it yields better results and saves time. This approach is more impactful than speeches and memos that try to enlist support for change. The LMC Process builds strong relationships, provides clarity for everyone about the direction, engages people in shaping the path forward, and helps leaders empower others so they want to support and participate in the change.

This case study illustrates the power of thoughtful leadership, exceptional teamwork, and conscious collaboration. As a small, passionate cohesive team, the senior leaders at the City of Ottawa were successful in creating a culture of One City, One Team by capturing the hearts, minds, and souls of the people they led, worked with, and served. They inspired thousands of city employees and an elected city council to embrace a mindset, values, and behaviors that continue to permeate across Ottawa at all levels of the organization and beyond.

The City of Ottawa SLT's story is inspiring. It calls us to reflect on our own approach to leading meaningful change. The SLT's courage, commitment, and dedication to a higher purpose as individuals, as leaders, and as a team bring to life the importance of understanding and being intentional about the choices we make in our Use-of-Self and the actions we take to lead change. Together, we can make a positive difference in our workplaces, communities, and society.

PART 2

The Leading Meaningful Change Toolkit

The LMC toolkit is designed to highlight some of the key exercises that you can use to put the concepts from part 1 into practice. The toolkit supplements the many exercises described in detail in chapters 2, 4, and 6 with additional exercises that were not elaborated on in the chapters. You can do these exercises on your own or as a team to

- deepen your understanding of what you need to lead meaningful change;
- develop and strengthen your change plan; and
- develop your competencies to lead and manage meaningful change.

Here is the list of all the essential exercises discussed in the book. You can refer back to the chapters for the exercises listed in regular typeface. The ten exercises in **boldface** are in this toolkit. Please customize and adapt these exercises to develop your approach to leading meaningful change.

Chapter 2: Six Keys to Guide Your Use-of-Self in the Leading Meaningful Change Process

- Choice Awareness Matrix
- Inspiring Leaders Exercise

- Reframing Exercise
- **Power Map Exercise**
- **Coaching Conversation Exercise**

Chapter 4: The Four Stages of the Leading Meaningful Change Process

- **Change Leadership Challenge Exercise**
- **Evaluating and Sustaining Meaningful Change Exercise**
- **Stakeholder Analysis Exercise**
- **Master Change Plan Exercise**
- **Developing a Communications Plan Exercise**

Chapter 6: Tools to Foster Teamwork, Collaboration, and Partnerships in Leading Meaningful Change

- Envisioning Success Exercise
- Team Charter Exercise
- **Change Leadership Competencies Exercise**
- **Assessing Your Personal Style of Managing Exercise**
- **Leading Meaningful Change Self-Development Guide**
- Gallery Walk Exercise
- Alignment Observation Tool

Power Map Exercise

This exercise is designed in eight steps to help you assess, understand, and develop strategies to navigate the formal and informal power dynamics that you may be experiencing in the LMC Process. An example of a power map follows the instructions.

Step 1: Pick a power challenge
Step 2: Map the people who are involved
Step 3: Map your relationships
Step 4: Map their relationships to you
Step 5: Map their relationships to each other

Step 6: Reflect on your power map

Step 7: Develop your action plan

Step 8: Develop a power map to understand the formal and informal networks

→ Step 1: Pick a Power Challenge

Think about your change process and select a power challenge or a struggle that you need to address. Here are some examples:

- Conflicting interests within the team are hindering the team's ability to implement change.
- As a leader, you are in conflict with one of your direct reports who is not providing you with the data and information you need, thus putting your project at risk.
- You need to influence your peers to be involved in the change process.
- You are told that the people on the front line don't understand the change. You need their collective support and commitment.

→ Step 2: Map the People Who Are Involved

Now that you have a challenge, draw your power map. At the end of this exercise is a sample that you can use.

1. Draw a circle at the top of the page and write your name in it.

2. Draw one circle for each person you interact with and who are involved in your scenario, and write their names in the circles. Each circle should have one name in it. These people may be members of your senior leadership team, direct reports, peers, or members of extended teams, networks, or informal groups.

→ Step 3: Map Your Relationships

Start with your circle and draw arrows from you to each person, using this legend for the type of arrow to draw to illustrate your relationship with them.

If you have six people, for example, you will have at least six arrows and possibly more.

Legend:
- Positive and supportive relationship one way
- Mutually positive and supportive relationship
- One-way conflict or tension in the relationship
- Mutual conflict or tension in the relationship
- No relationship (no line)

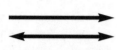

→ Step 4: Map Their Relationships to You

Use the same legend and draw arrows from each person to your circle to illustrate their relationship to you.

→ Step 5: Map Their Relationships to Each Other

Use the same legend and draw arrows between the other people's circles to show their relationships to each other.

→ Step 6: Reflect on Your Power Map

Here are four types of power and some questions to help you reflect on your use of power and the power dynamics that you need to navigate in your scenario:

Personal Power	Formal Power	Informal Power	Collective Power
• Personal charm and charisma • Expertise, achievements, and influence • Wisdom	• Roles • Responsibilities • Accountabilities and structures • Processes • Procedures	• Informal relationships • Friends • Family • Colleagues • Shared interests inside and outside the organization	• Membership in communities of practice • Professional networks • Associations • Political and strategic partnerships

1. What does your power map tell you? Are there any surprises?

2. With whom do you have positive and supportive relationships? Why?

3. Are there cliques, alliances, pairings, or silos that are helping or hindering your ability to advance your plan? What are their interests, concerns, and fears? Who supports your work? Are you part of or excluded from any partnerships, teams, or alliances that are important for you to get your work done?

4. Are these the relationships you need for success? Who is missing? Who is not involved and needs to be? Are there relationships that you can build or strengthen to help you influence others?

5. Who are you having difficulty working with? Who is resisting? Who are their supporters?

6. With whom are you or others experiencing tension or conflict? Why? (Go back to question 3.)

7. What are your strengths and challenges using personal, formal, informal, and collective power?

8. What types of power are you using that are effective? What can you modify, adapt, learn, or develop? What types of power are you underusing? How is this working for you? Where are you blocked or stuck?

9. What supports do you need? Are there informal networks or people that you need to tap into for support?

10. What can you do to be more effective navigating these power dynamics?

→ Step 7: Develop Your Action Plan

1. What are your next steps?
2. What choices and assumptions are influencing your approach to dealing with these power dynamics?
3. What types of power do you need to be effective?
4. How are you empowering yourself and others?
5. How are you disempowering yourself and others?

→ Step 8: Develop a Power Map to Understand the Formal and Informal Networks

This step is an extra one. You can use the same approach and develop a power map of the formal and informal networks that are connected to the people in your first map. This may include the extended team, stakeholders, networks, and informal groups.

Example

Scenario: Charles, the new vice president, strategy, was responsible for implementing a project management process to support an innovation initiative in his organization. He was having difficulty getting buy-in for the new process and developing a shared vision with his project team. He discovered a lot of power dynamics were at play, so he completed a power map to help him develop a strategy to address the conflicts and build a cohesive team. As you can see in Diagram 1, Charles has a mutually positive and supportive relationship with George and Jane. These three team members are aligned.

But look at Charles's relationships with the other members of the team in Diagram 2. There is mutual tension and conflict between Charles and Henry, and between Jean and Henry. Jean and Phillip are also in conflict. While these conflicts exist, Charles also realizes that he has no relationship with Jean or Phillip, as there are no lines from him to them.

Diagram 1 Alignment

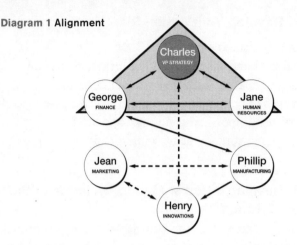

There is one outlier: a positive relationship from Phillip to Henry. Perhaps Charles can leverage this to help him build his relationship with Henry.

Diagram 2 Conflicts

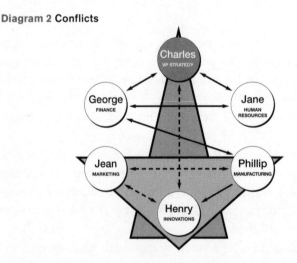

In Diagram 3, there appears to be two teams within the team, and no relationships between George and Jean, Jane and Jean, or Jane and Phillip. Charles needs to develop strategies to break down these walls and get the team working together toward a shared vision.

Diagram 3 Silos

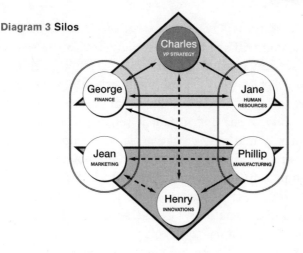

Action plan: At first glance, Charles may notice some opportunities to leverage his formal and informal power to build relationships. As the leader of the project team, he is accountable for developing a cohesive team and implementing the new process. He may want to bring the team together and develop strategies to help them work more effectively together (formal power).

Since he is new, he may also want to build trust with each team member. He could check into their interests, such as sports or local interests, and make arrangements to attend an event together. To break the silos, he could organize an evening at a ball game to help people get to know each other better. These activities would help Charles model his teamwork values and what he expects from the team (personal power).

This map also shines the light on the negative impact that the conflict between Charles and Henry is having on the team. Charles may need to reach out to Henry and build a more constructive working relationship with him (formal power).

Since Charles and Henry are not communicating with each other, Charles could also informally seek advice and support from Phillip, who has a positive relationship with Henry, to find out what Henry's issues and concerns are (informal power).

Now, looking at Charles's extended relationships in Diagram 4, you will see that he is aligned with the senior leadership team (formal power) and academic partners. He is also very active as a board member at the university (collective power). However, he needs to work on his relationship with the board, as it is tense (formal power). He also has a mutually negative relationship with the industry trade association (collective power). These relationships will be important for advancing his work. Henry shares these concerns, as he is very active with the board and associations. Given these insights, Charles could work with Henry to develop a plan to build these relationships and address his concerns. This would help Charles to gain Henry's trust and confidence in the plan, which would hopefully resolve the conflict.

Diagram 4 Relationships to Build

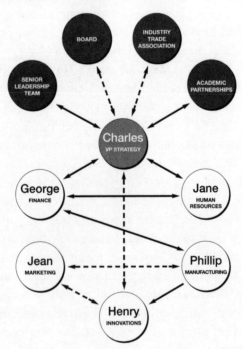

Coaching Conversation Exercise

This exercise is designed to help you prepare for a five-minute coaching conversation from three points of view: the coach (the leader or manager needing to coach someone), the coachee, and the observer. This process will also help you learn from each other about how to give and receive feedback and develop your coaching competencies.

Select a topic for the coaching conversation that is meaningful to you and that will help you overcome some obstacles to your success in leading and managing change. Here are some examples of coaching conversations that you can use as a guide to develop your own scenario:

- *Coaching direct reports:* Your direct report is having difficulty working with the staff from another department. This has created conflict between the individuals who need to work together to ensure the handoff from one department to another goes smoothly and doesn't negatively impact the client experience. How do you want to approach this coaching conversation?

- *Coaching or influencing without formal authority, peer to peer:* Your peer is blocking your work or is not quite on board with your plan. This is having an impact on your work. How do you want to approach this peer-to-peer coaching conversation with your colleague so you can develop more effective ways of working together?

- *Coaching-influencing upward:* You need to provide some difficult feedback to a senior leader following a meeting with key stakeholders that did not go so well. How do you want to approach this scenario? What do you want to say or do?

→ **Instructions for the Coach**

If you are taking on the role of the coach, review these questions and explain to both your coachee and the observer what you would like feedback on as you have this coaching conversation.

Part 1: Coaching Context: Describe Your Coaching Conversation Scenario

1. Who does it involve? Where does it take place?
2. What does success look like for you and the other person in the conversation?
3. What are your intentions?
4. Why is this conversation important to you? The other person? Your department? The client?

Learning Goals

1. What do you need to be at your best during this conversation?
2. How will you use your strengths as a leader and/or coach in this situation?
3. What challenges or learning opportunities do you want to work on?
4. What do you want the observer and coach to pay attention to or give you feedback on as they observe your interaction in this coaching conversation?

Part 2: Reflect on How You Did in the Coaching Conversation

1. What went well in your coaching conversation?
2. What strengths did you discover or affirm?
3. Where were you challenged?
4. What might you do differently next time?
5. How successful were you in building an effective relationship with your coachee?

6. Were you able to accomplish your intentions? If so, what did you do to be successful?

7. How well did you follow the coaching conversation structure?

   ☐ Check in

   ☐ Define the purpose

   ☐ Review objectives and actions from previous session

   ☐ Identify successes and learning opportunities

   ☐ Develop an action plan

   ☐ Check out

   ☐ Follow up

→ Instructions for the Coachee

If you are the person being coached, answer these questions to help you reflect on your coaching experience:

1. How was your experience in this coaching conversation?
2. What did your coach do well?
3. What did the coach do that was effective in building your relationship?
4. How did you feel? Were you heard and understood?
5. What could the coach do differently to enhance your conversation?

→ Instructions for the Observer

If you are the observer, answer these questions to provide feedback to the coach:

1. How well did the coach follow the coaching conversation structure?

   ☐ Check in

   ☐ Define the purpose

☐ Review objectives and actions from previous session

☐ Identify successes and learning opportunities

☐ Develop an action plan

☐ Check out

☐ Follow up

2. What did the coach do well?
3. What did you observe about the coach that addresses their original request for feedback and their objectives?
4. What could the coach do differently to enhance the coaching conversation?
5. How did the coach help the coachee to understand the issues and commit to a mutually agreed-upon solution or action plan?

Change Leadership Challenge Exercise

This exercise is designed to provide you with an opportunity to reflect on your approach to leading meaningful change. First review the guidelines and examples to help you select your change leadership challenge topic. Once you have your topic, move on to complete the change leadership challenge outline.

→ Guidelines

1. Select a project that you are currently working on or are about to launch to ground your learning and put into practice the theories, concepts, and tools of the LMC Framework.
2. Don't worry about having all the answers to the questions. This exercise is a living document that you will modify and adapt as you develop and implement your plan.

3. You can complete this exercise on your own or as part of a team.
4. Your change leadership challenge must be work that is real and in your span of authority or control.

→ Examples

Here are some examples of change leadership challenges to help you identify your topic for this exercise:

1. Developing a process to create a shared vision for a department, a service area, or your entire organization
2. Determining strategies to deal with resistance as you develop or implement a new business process, organizational structure, or technology system
3. Developing a process to create alignment, commitment, or support from key leaders and stakeholders
4. Motivating people to come out of their silos and collaborate across the organization
5. Developing strategies to lead and manage a culture shift that involves transforming the traditional organization to a digital workplace
6. Developing ways to be more effective dealing with conflict and political dynamics
7. Learning how to inspire, communicate, and engage others throughout the change process
8. Any other challenges that are relevant for you

→ Your Change Leadership Challenge

Title:

1. Describe your change project or leadership challenge:

This can be a specific project or initiative that is in your span of control and that you are currently responsible for leading and managing.

a. What is the context (factors influencing the change: internal and external forces for and/or against the change)?

b. Why is it important to address this project or challenge at this time?
c. What are the objectives, deliverables, and expected outcomes?
d. Who are the key stakeholders who need to be involved in the change?
e. How will you measure success?

2. Describe the anticipated impacts of the change on the
a. people
b. culture
c. process
d. technology
e. structure

3. Provide an overview of your project or initiative:
a. Where are you in your project plan?
b. What key milestones and results have you achieved?
c. What successes have you achieved?
d. What is helping you to be successful?
e. What are your challenges or learning opportunities?
f. Where are you blocked, stalled, or needing some assistance?
g. What is preventing you from being as successful as you would like to be?
h. How ready are your key stakeholders to participate and engage in the change process?

4. Describe your learning goals and objectives:
a. Where are you having the most success leading and managing your change leadership challenge?
b. Where are you having the most difficulty?
c. What impact do you want or need to have for success?
d. What are your goals and objectives?
e. What key questions or hot topics would you like to address that would be most helpful to you and your team in developing your change plan or strategy?

→ **Example**

Here is an example of one manager's change leadership challenge.

Change Leadership Challenge: Leading the Implementation of a New Compensation System

1. Describe your change project or leadership challenge:

We are currently in the process of changing our compensation structure to move from a seniority-based system to a performance-based system. Our organization has been using our current compensation structure for decades. Salary increases are based on seniority, years of service. We are experiencing significant growth and cannot afford our current model. We are falling behind our competitors and are losing our ability to attract the best talent because we can't afford to match our competitors. Our current compensation model is not sustainable. In order to be more cost-competitive, high-performing, and a sustainable organization, the decision was made to align our compensation structure with the best practices within our industry. Our approach includes two phases and impacts all managers and employees.

Deliverables:

Phase 1: Understand and evaluate the current compensation model

1. Move to a job evaluation system that is more widely used within our industry.
2. Evaluate all positions that are affected within the new system.
3. Align all these roles within the new salary bands.
4. Develop and execute a change management plan that includes communications about the new structure and impact on employees.

Phase 2: Design the new compensation model

1. Develop and implement key performance indicators (KPIs) for all roles.
2. Develop a new performance evaluation system.
3. Develop a new compensation model and administration guidelines and process.
4. Develop and execute a change management plan that includes training and communications on the new compensation model and process.

2. Describe the anticipated impacts of the change:
People:
Managers will have more accountability in the compensation process. They will be required to actively manage performance with targets and deliverables. This will require monitoring, developing, and evaluating employee performance and business results. Managers will need to develop skills in having difficult conversations with employees as they justify performance ratings and salary increases.

Culture:
The new compensation program will have an impact on the organization's culture at the manager and employee levels. Currently, employees receive salary increases regardless of performance. Going forward, salary increases will be tied to employee performance, advancement, and succession planning. These changes will move the organization away from a culture of entitlement to pay for performance.

Process and technology:
The human resources (HR) team will need to align this project with the new human resources information system (HRIS) that will be launched in the next year. This project will bring changes in the way we conduct

performance appraisals. Ratings will be completed online, allowing for easy access and better administration of the compensation program. In addition to a new compensation process, managers and the HR team will need to be trained on how to complete performance evaluations in the new HRIS.

Structure:
There will be a new HR structure that includes changes in roles and responsibilities. There will be HR advisors who will be involved in more strategic, less tactical work. Managers will take on more responsibilities in the performance management process and be restricted in how they can financially reward their people. Employees will also need to use technology to access HR information and rely less on direct contact with an HR agent. Development to lead and manage this significant change will be required for all employees.

3. Provide an overview of your project or initiative:
Phase 1 is almost completed. All jobs within the organization have been evaluated under the new job evaluation system and aligned to the new salary bands. All employees were advised of their new salary bands. A change management plan was developed and implemented for phase 1 and introduced to the managers.

The change impacted a significant number of employees who no longer were eligible for salary increases due to where their position sits in the new salary bands. As you can imagine, some managers are angry and not supporting the changes. They are resisting because they do not think the new system is fair. Their salaries are reduced. Some employees even lost their automatic cost of living increase. In addition, staff expressed concern that the changes in our compensation structure are an indicator that we are losing our small-company feel and becoming a large machine.

Our new structure is making it more difficult to recruit for contract roles in some areas where significant experience is required. Our managers are not used to losing candidates due to salary expectations or having to hire a candidate with less than the desired level of experience. Some managers are finding the adjustment difficult.

Phase 2 is underway and managers are rolling out KPIs as part of our new compensation program. Based on the managers' feedback, they are telling us they need more coaching and support on how to discuss the changes with their staff. Changes that impact compensation are never easy and managers need to be more comfortable with engaging their employees in these difficult conversations.

4. Describe your learning goals and objectives:
Over the next two years, we need to lead and manage these significant culture shifts. We want to be intentional in ensuring we maintain the best parts of our culture while we address our short-term needs and remain sustainable for the long term. The change to our compensation, shifting from entitlement to pay for performance, is only one of several changes the organization will undergo in the next few years. Personally, I need to understand more about leading and managing people through change. I also need tools to understand the organizational culture and paradigm shifts and how to create a master change plan to effectively lead and manage this change leadership challenge.

Evaluating and Sustaining Meaningful Change Exercise

This exercise is best done as a team. It is designed to walk you through each stage of the LMC Framework—alignment, integration, action, and renewal—so you can reflect on and evaluate the effectiveness of your LMC Process, develop your next steps, and increase your potential to sustain the culture shifts you need for long-term success.

→ **Instructions**

1. Review your change plan.
2. Answer the questions on the following pages to assess the impact you are having at each stage of the LMC Process.
3. Fill out the checklists for each stage to assess how complete your change effort is.
4. Based on the checklists and questions, are there ideas or strategies that you need to add to your plan? What actions might you need to take to enhance your plan and create the highest potential for success?

→ **Stage 1: Alignment**

This stage focuses on creating alignment on the strategic priorities, purpose, vision, and values that will guide the change journey. The goal of this stage is to ensure that leaders at all levels of the organization understand their role and the context for change, and plan how they will work together to lead and manage the journey. Here are some questions to help you assess alignment:

1. How are you creating alignment on the need for change and developing a shared purpose, vision, and values?
2. Do you have alignment with the people who need to help you or who will be impacted by the change? Do you have their commitment and support for the plan?
3. Why is this change important? What is the benefit of the change for your employees, clients, and stakeholders?

4. How will people find meaning in the change? What will motivate them to be involved in supporting the change?
5. How does your change align with and support your organization's vision, purpose, and strategic priorities? Are there synergies or disconnects?
6. What culture shifts do you need to make?
7. Who needs to be involved to lead and manage your plan? Are they informed, engaged, and participating? Is there any resistance?

→ Stage 2: Integration

The focus of this stage is on creating opportunities for people to develop the skills, tools, and supports for their own learning and development as they go through the change process. Grounding the plan, tools, and techniques with real-life examples using people's real work will facilitate the process. Here are some questions to assess integration:

1. How are you integrating the purpose, values, principles, and behaviors in your strategy or plan?
2. How are you leading, managing, and communicating your plan?
3. What actions can you take to ensure people understand the relationship and impact of the change to their work?
4. What processes and structures do you have in place to develop people to lead, manage, and participate in the change process?
5. Do you have a way to measure how well you and others are integrating their learning and the changes in their day-to-day work?
6. How can you customize the tools and approach to guide and communicate the change so they are easy for people to grasp and apply in their work?

→ Stage 3: Action

The focus of the action stage is to participate in a continuous and dynamic cycle of action, reflection, and learning as you develop and implement the plan. Here are some questions to assess action:

1. How are you living the purpose, mindset, values, and behaviors as you put your plan into action?
2. How are you tracking the planned and emerging themes, trends, and issues that may influence your change plan?
3. What culture shifts are needed for success?
4. What actions are you incorporating in your plan to achieve these changes?
5. How effectively are you communicating, engaging, and collaborating with others?
6. What are your personal leadership challenge and development priorities going forward?

→ Stage 4: Renewal

The focus of the renewal phase is to conduct an overall evaluation of the change process. This evaluation should be done at critical milestones, at the completion of the project, and/or just before you begin the next phase of work in the LMC Process. Here are some questions to assess the renewal stage:

1. Are you achieving your desired results and impacts?
2. How are you evaluating and measuring the impact of your plan?
3. Do you need to work with other people, projects, or initiatives to advance your plan and achieve your desired results?
4. Do you need to manage any risks to ensure the highest probability of success?

Stage 1: To assess alignment, check off the elements you have in place.	Strategies for next steps
☐ Engaged champion(s) and leader(s) to actively lead the change	☐ Identify credible and engaged champion(s) and leader(s) to actively lead and engage others in the change. ☐ Form a design team to lead and manage alignment.
☐ A shared understanding of the need for change	☐ Develop a process to create a common awareness and understanding of the need for change. ☐ Have people observe other parts of the organization to gain empathy and understanding of complex issues, resistance, and other factors that influence their positions.
☐ Clarity, commitment, and alignment regarding the purpose, vision, and priorities for the change, and the principles, values, and behaviors that will guide it with • the executive team • middle management • the front line • clients • political stakeholders • partners • other stakeholders • the community	☐ Conduct consultations with internal stakeholders. ☐ Conduct consultations with external stakeholders. ☐ Hold forums to discuss observations and respond to feedback or suggestions. ☐ Share examples and best/wise practices. ☐ Show how the concepts and best/wise practices apply to your context. ☐ Develop stories that illustrate where you are headed.

☐ An effective governance and organizational design that outlines accountabilities, delegated authorities, and decision-making processes that are defined, understood, and followed	☐ Develop a governance structure. ☐ Develop an organizational design and structures to support change.
☐ An understanding of the executive/leadership team's role and contribution to the change process	☐ Clarify roles and responsibilities. ☐ Provide training and development. ☐ Coach and mentor. ☐ Hold forums and working sessions with the team.
☐ Meaningful participation from all relevant stakeholders: <ul><li>internal stakeholders</li><li>external stakeholders</li><li>partners</li></ul>	☐ Design working sessions that are meaningful and provide opportunity for learning, input, decision making, and teamwork. ☐ Develop a strategy to develop leaders to lead and manage change.
☐ Defined language to guide your communications at all levels of the organization and beyond	☐ Provide direction, guiding principles, tools, and supports for communication. ☐ Develop a lexicon. ☐ Develop tools and supports, such as videos, websites, online surveys, etc.
☐ Teamwork and collaboration where required	☐ Develop key messages as a team. ☐ Apply any of the previously mentioned strategies.

STAGE 1
2/2

Stage 2: To assess integration, check off the elements you have in place.	Strategies for next steps
☐ A baseline to measure how well you and others are doing throughout the change process, including: • pace of change • progress on your plan, deadlines, and commitments • successes and challenges • skill development • adoption of change • culture shifts	☐ Develop, implement, and monitor the plan. ☐ Put in place program/project management principles, methodology, and process. ☐ Develop and implement an evaluation process. ☐ Share feedback, observations, and emergent actions and impacts of the change plan with the design team and use the observations to advance, enhance, or modify the strategy and plan. ☐ Communicate and reinforce performance targets, timelines, deliverables, commitments, and expected outcomes.
☐ Customized materials, examples, tools, and processes that help employees understand and integrate the concepts and changes in their work ☐ Customized stories that demonstrate successful changes or movement in the desired direction ☐ Integration of the purpose, principles, and values to guide and communicate the change, including language, materials, and methods	☐ Customize the change program design, tools, and supports for learning and integration in real work. ☐ Develop a lexicon that describes the new terms, abbreviations, and concepts. ☐ Provide concrete examples.

☐ An approach to measure and evaluate the executive and/or leadership team's development and impact throughout the change process

☐ Hold regular checkpoint meetings with senior management/ leadership teams and relevant stakeholders to educate them or develop their understanding of the plan, results, and expectations of them to continue leading and managing the culture shifts.

☐ Review communications to ensure integration and consistency.

☐ Communicate successes.

☐ Reflect on stakeholders and where there are challenges, and develop strategies to address their concerns.

☐ Coach upward, with peers, and across the department and organization.

☐ Use the data to develop more empowering strategies that work and are relevant for your culture.

☐ Conduct a stakeholder analysis and develop strategies to reinforce mindsets and behaviors.

☐ Follow up with people to address their concerns and resistance and to explain the change.

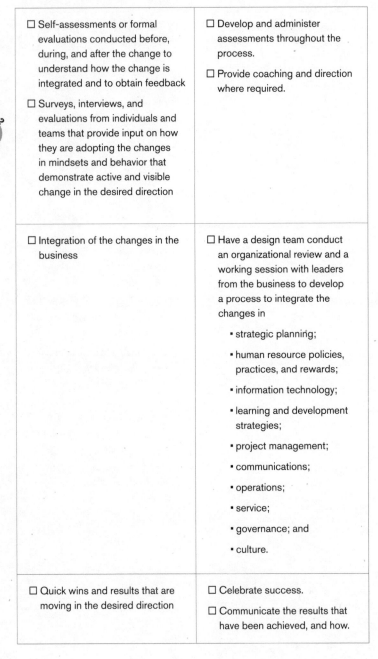

☐ Self-assessments or formal evaluations conducted before, during, and after the change to understand how the change is integrated and to obtain feedback ☐ Surveys, interviews, and evaluations from individuals and teams that provide input on how they are adopting the changes in mindsets and behavior that demonstrate active and visible change in the desired direction	☐ Develop and administer assessments throughout the process. ☐ Provide coaching and direction where required.

☐ Integration of the changes in the business	☐ Have a design team conduct an organizational review and a working session with leaders from the business to develop a process to integrate the changes in
	
	   • strategic planning;
	   • human resource policies, practices, and rewards;
	   • information technology;
	   • learning and development strategies;
	   • project management;
	   • communications;
	   • operations;
	   • service;
	   • governance; and
	   • culture.

☐ Quick wins and results that are moving in the desired direction	☐ Celebrate success. ☐ Communicate the results that have been achieved, and how.

Stage 3: To assess action, check off the elements you have in place.	Strategies for next steps
☐ An approach to track themes and patterns from shared experiences, actions, and learning	☐ Develop and implement a process to track themes and patterns from shared experiences, actions, and learning over time.
☐ Measures to assess the culture shifts ☐ Meaningful feedback from meetings and pulse checks	☐ Track and monitor how the desired mindsets, values, and behaviors are being lived inside the organization, with partners and stakeholders, and in the community. ☐ Provide tools and checklists. ☐ Tell stories to enhance learning, reinforce the culture shifts, and demonstrate mindset, values, behaviors, and competencies required for success. ☐ Provide models and wise practices based on current, real-life examples of successful projects and the lessons, concepts, and tools that can be replicated across the organization.
☐ Delegated accountabilities and formal and informal power structures that are clearly understood and acted upon at all levels	☐ Create a common understanding of the reasons for the changes and the complex cultural and power dynamics that need to be honored, challenged, or changed.
☐ An understanding of your Use-of-Self and the impact of your actions on what was implemented, changed, or adapted	☐ Establish personal leadership development goals and action plans that include resources and support systems to draw on for growth and success.

STAGE 3
1/2

□ Individual and/or team development plans

□ Self-rating and/or formal assessments of the individual or team to assess mindset, competencies, and behaviors

□ Behavioral measures to assess the adoption of change

□ Insights and experiences from personal leadership reflection questions and journals

□ Frequency and quality of participation in coaching and mentoring discussions

□ Quantity and quality of reflections and impacts reported in project team meetings and informally between structured learning and working sessions

□ Obtain a baseline of the individual and/or team leadership profile.

□ Review results of assessments.

□ Identify common leadership strengths and challenges.

□ Track performance and progress over time.

□ Develop learning and development plans for the individual and/or team.

□ Provide individual and/or team coaching, mentoring, and learning and development activities.

Stage 4: To assess renewal, check off the elements you have in place.

Strategies for next steps

□ A process to monitor, measure, benchmark, and report on the plan, results, and impacts achieved (people, business, financial, time, quality, process, service, and product improvements)

□ Implement a process to review all strategic and operational plans to ensure the purpose, priorities, and impacts are understood by all the people involved in the change.

□ Review all plans to ensure the purpose and the priorities that cross over all services or functions are reflected in the operational plans.

□ Review objectives, provide an update on strategic/operational plans, and assess progress and results.

- ☐ Culture shifts that are embedded as a way of working and incorporated in
  - behaviors
  - day-to-day operations
  - service delivery
  - product development
  - policies and procedures
  - checkpoint meetings
  - annual and quarterly reports
  - manager forums
  - training and development activities
  - presentations
  - other aspects of the business
- ☐ Reviews, surveys, and pulse checks that demonstrate increased confidence, satisfaction, and positive feedback from
  - senior management
  - leaders
  - managers
  - direct reports
  - operations
  - political and governing stakeholders
  - clients
  - partners
  - others
- ☐ A process to communicate success stories and lessons learned

- ☐ Conduct a reflection process to deepen the understanding of the culture shifts, impacts, and results and how they were achieved.
- ☐ Continue or make adjustments to the plan.
- ☐ Assess stakeholders' understanding and adoption of change at all levels of the organization.
- ☐ Assess how effectively people are using their formal and informal networks.
- ☐ Develop ways to learn and build on ideas from other areas and departments.
- ☐ Develop strategies to increase employee engagement.
- ☐ Develop rewards strategies to support the culture shifts.
- ☐ Develop strategies to increase client satisfaction.
- ☐ Develop strategies to increase operational excellence.
- ☐ Increase the breadth, depth, and scope of the project.
- ☐ Transfer knowledge and learn from wise practices being used in other places.

STAGE 4

2/3

☐ Qualitative and quantitative measurements of the impact of the changes on employees' health and well-being, performance, and/or learning	☐ Assess pace and adoption of change and adjust accordingly. ☐ Review staff turnover, sick leaves, and health and wellness data to foster a healthy workplace.
☐ Strategies, plans, and projects to sustain change, innovate, and go to the next steps	☐ Develop customized supports, coaching, and mentoring for people struggling to implement the culture shifts.

STAGE 3/3

→ **Action Plan**

Based on the results of the questions and checklists above, what should you focus on next?

1. What needs to be modified, adapted, or incorporated in your Master Change Plan?
2. What does the team need to do to advance this work?
3. Who else might need to be involved?

Stakeholder Analysis Exercise

This stakeholder analysis will help you assess where your stakeholders are in the LMC Process and develop an action plan to help them adapt and move through the change process.

→ **Step 1: Stakeholder Analysis**

In the grid opposite, list your stakeholders at the top of each column; you can either use their name or their title. Then, using the legend below the grid, mark a check mark, a circle, or an x to indicate the status of each stakeholder for each stage of the LMC Process. Are your stakeholders where you need them to be?

An example of a completed grid is shown on page 226. (If you prefer, you can use people's real names instead of their functions. For example, you can write "Jane, head of IT," "Richard, head of operations," etc.) As you can see in this example, the executives and directors are on track, the managers are not fully supporting the change, and front-line staff are resisting the change. All stakeholders are on track for the renewal stage because they are not yet at this point of the LMC Process.

Stakeholders				
Stage of LMC Process	Name	Name	Name	Name
Alignment				
Integration				
Action				
Renewal				

Legend:

On track	Caution	Needs action
✓ Stakeholders are on track and demonstrating the right level of understanding and involvement for this phase of change. ✓ Continue with your plan.	O Stakeholders are not fully supporting the change. O Reach out and provide support.	☒ Stakeholders are not demonstrating the desired behaviors and supports needed at this stage of change. ☒ Develop action plans to increase their understanding of and sense of urgency for the change. ☒ Reach out and find out why they are resisting. ☒ Develop customized strategies for each stakeholder group.

Stage of LMC Process	Executives	Directors	Managers	Front Line
Alignment	✓	✓	○	☒
Integration	✓	✓	○	☒
Action	✓	✓	○	☒
Renewal	✓	✓	✓	✓

→ Step 2: Stakeholder Analysis Action Plan

In this grid, identify further details about each stakeholder's status and reflect on what technical, political, and symbolic strategies and skills you can employ to mitigate any resistance and concerns. (Add more rows as needed.)

Who are your stakeholders?	What types of resistance are they demonstrating? • Cognitive • Ideological • Power • Psychological	What are their motivations, issues, and concerns?	What strategies can you use to obtain their support and engagement in the change process? • Technical • Political • Symbolic

Master Change Plan Exercise

→ **Objectives**

The Master Change Plan will help you align your project plan, priorities, and supports with your organization's larger purpose and strategic priorities. Use the grid below or make a spreadsheet similar to it.

Q_ Where do you expect to be in the change process?	Q_ Where do you expect to be in the change process?	Q_ Where do you expect to be in the change process?	Q_ Where do you expect to be in the change process?
CORPORATE Identify the corporate milestones, activities, and interdependencies that will influence your project and change plan. Monthly/Quarterly Report • Quarterly Production Forecast • Quarterly Cost Forecast • Board Meeting			
PROJECT Identify the key milestones, activities, and interdependencies that will be addressed in your project plan.			
SUPPORTS What structures, processes, leadership development, networks, and supports will people need to build the competencies to lead/manage this change/project?			
COMMUNICATIONS What key milestones, processes, and supports do people need to effectively communicate, understand, and engage with your plan?			

Chapter 4 (pages 108–13) provides detailed instructions on using this tool, but briefly, here is how to fill out the grid:

Timeline and Change Journey Rows
The columns in the grid reflect your timeline. Depending on your project, you might use the business cycle of quarters (Q1, Q2, Q3, Q4) or a monthly timeline (in which case you will need 12 columns).

Using the timeline you decide on, write down in each column of the second row an answer to the question, "Where do you expect to be in the change process?" To answer the question, use the four-stage LMC Process. For example, are you creating alignment, planning for integration, taking action to implement and/or evaluate change, or renewing it?

Corporate and Project Rows
In the corporate row, you identify the corporate or institutional milestones, decision points, activities, or the interdependencies that you need to consider and that will influence your projects and change plans. These activities may include checkpoint meetings like monthly or quarterly executive meetings. They may also include summary reports, production forecasts, and/or board or council meetings.

Most people start developing their Master Change Plans in the project row of the chart because their project is already underway and they often have a project plan. However, these projects are sometimes not aligned and integrated with the larger organizational strategy. In the project area, map the key milestones, activities, and interdependencies that will be addressed in your project plan.

Supports Row
In this row, identify the structures, processes, leadership development activities, networks, and other supports that people will need to build the competencies for leading and managing their project. Supports may include new

task teams or project teams, participation from executive members, or specific leadership and technical development activities to build new skills or implement new technologies and processes.

Communications Row
This is where you review your project plan and identify the key milestones, processes, and supports you need to help you communicate with and engage others. This row usually presents opportunities to make use of and streamline existing corporate and departmental communication methods, products, and processes. It also helps to identify what needs to be communicated and when and how to approach stakeholders, especially when an organization is undergoing significant change. Mapping your communications activities helps you collaborate more effectively and efficiently by making more visible what, why, how, and when communication needs to happen and who needs to be involved.

→ When to Create Your Master Change Plan
You can develop a Master Change Plan for one specific project or for each of the multiple projects supporting larger corporate initiatives or transformations. The timeline can also be extended depending on the complexity of your change strategy. There is a lot of value in doing this exercise with multiple projects and stakeholders to identify synergies, create alignment, and build better focus and capacity to lead and manage your plans.

→ The Master Change Plan Workshop
In many larger organization-wide change initiatives, we conduct a one-day Master Change Plan Workshop for leaders or teams from business functions and/or from other change projects or initiatives. Prior to the session, we usually ask people to complete their project plans. The plans are then posted on the wall during the workshop for everyone

to view and discuss. We then look at what we are observing and learning to

- identify and understand patterns, such as what is on all plans and what is missing;
- understand the organization's culture and what needs to be honored or needs to shift or change;
- find synergies, dependencies, and interdependencies across the organization;
- test the feasibility of the plan and set the priorities and sequencing of activities and the pace of change;
- identify ways to work more efficiently and productively by reducing duplication and sharing resources; and
- build and strengthen internal partnerships, teamwork, and cross-company collaboration as different teams complete their individual Master Change Plans and their project plans.

Here are some questions to help guide this discussion:

1. What observations and insights do I have related to the guiding principles and priorities for the change?

2. What additional opportunities do I see for alignment, synergies, efficiencies, and collaboration?

3. What are the people, strategies, and actions that are interdependent and/or dependent on some of my department or service area's deliverables?

4. What resources do I need to share or make use of to build capacity and focus for success?

5. What ideas can I leverage or integrate in my department or service area's plan?

6. What feedback do I need to give to my colleagues or specific teams or departments?

7. See the recommendations in chapter 4 (pages 114–15) for avoiding some common pitfalls when using and presenting the Master Change Plan.

Developing a Communications Plan Exercise

This exercise is designed to help you develop a communications plan to support your change. Please follow these steps to complete the exercise.

1. Experience the communications process as a member of an audience
2. Develop guiding principles and key messages
3. Understand the needs of your audience
4. Develop and practice doing an elevator or coffee conversation
5. Develop a communications plan

→ Step 1: Experience the Communications Process as a Member of an Audience

Attend a presentation on change or an all-staff meeting or forum in your organization. As a member of the audience, notice how the presenter communicates. Consider these questions:

1. Who was the target audience for this presentation?
2. What was the presenter's goal and key message?
3. How did the presenter set the stage for the presentation (podium, stage, teleprompter, physical setup)?
4. What messages are you picking up about the presenter's Use-of-Self, such as tone of voice, body language, values, and beliefs?
5. How did the presenter use key messages and guiding principles?

6. How did the presenter communicate a plan or use data, stories, analogies, metaphors, or images to communicate?
7. Notice how you are feeling. What emotions surfaced for you? Are you inspired and committed to action? Are you tuned out, bored, or concerned?
8. What did the presenter do that evoked these emotions in you and possibly in others?
9. How did you feel at the end of the presentation? Did the presenter achieve their objectives?
10. What advice would you give the presenter?
11. What insights will you incorporate in your communications going forward?

→ Step 2: Develop Guiding Principles and Key Messages

Here are some questions to consider as you develop your key messages:

1. What principles and values are going to guide your change journey?
2. Why is this change needed?
3. Do you have a plan? If so, do you have confidence in it? If not, what is your plan to develop the plan?
4. What will change, is changing, or has changed?
5. When is the change going to happen, start, or stop?
6. Who will be involved in or impacted by the change?
7. How are you going to lead and manage this change?
8. How do you feel about talking about the change?
9. What is the impact of the change on people, your service or product, or the community?

→ Step 3: Understand the Needs of Your Audience

Review the types of resistance and identify the motivations, issues, and concerns of your stakeholders. Based on what you are learning, what messages and strategies do you need to incorporate in your communications plan? (Add more rows as needed.)

Who are your stakeholders?	What types of resistance are they demonstrating? • Cognitive • Ideological • Power • Psychological	What are their motivations, issues, and concerns?	What strategies can you use to obtain their support and engagement in the change process? • Technical • Political • Symbolic

→ Step 4: Develop and Practice Doing an Elevator or Coffee Conversation

An elevator or coffee conversation is clear, short, and to the point. The goal is to send an easy-to-understand message about your vision and need for change. It is meant to

- help you synthesize and distill the essence of your change challenge so it's easy to understand and communicate to others;
- create alignment with people who are leading and managing the change by sending a uniform message that can be customized for your stakeholder audiences;
- provide an opportunity to promote your change and educate others, and for them to educate you; and
- provide an opportunity for you to learn from your stakeholders about what they need to help, support, and commit to the vision and change.

Here are a few guidelines to help you develop your elevator or coffee conversation:

- Review your results from steps 2 and 3.

- Be clear and precise about the name of your change challenge and/or your vision for the changes.
- Define the issue, problem, and/or goal you are trying to achieve.
- Explain what's in it for them (WIIFT) as a motivator for your audience so they will become interested and want to know more.
- Leave room for your audience to respond.

Practice Exercise

1. Select a stakeholder or stakeholder group and imagine that you are taking a two-minute elevator ride with them or standing around the coffee counter.
2. What questions or concerns about your change challenge do you anticipate they may have for you?
3. Develop a two-minute conversation that helps you address their concerns and communicates what your vision or change challenge is about.
4. Practice your conversation with your colleagues so they can give you feedback.

→ Step 5: Develop a Communications Plan

Review your change plan and strategy and complete the communications planning tool. (Add more rows as needed.)

Target Audience: Groups and Individuals	Commu- nication Activity	Methods and Tools	Require- ments	Responsi- bility	Date and Frequency

Change Leadership Competencies Exercise

This exercise is organized in two parts. The first part is a reflection exercise that builds on your previous experiences leading meaningful change. The second part is a self-assessment that you can do based on your reflections or using your current work.

→ **Part 1: Reflecting on Leading Large-Scale Change**

1. Reflect on a time when you led (or participated in the team that led) a large-scale change that required a shift in your organization's culture.

- How did you ensure the strategy you designed was aligned with the organization's purpose, vision, and strategic priorities? What was the context (internal and external, global and local) that influenced your approach?

- How did you engage the key stakeholders and create buy-in for your vision? What were the key challenges or resistance that you faced? How did you overcome these challenges? How successful were you and your team in leading and managing this culture shift?

2. Now think of a time when you were successful collaborating and building partnerships with stakeholders that were not originally aligned and possibly had divergent or competing interests from you and your team or department.

- Why was it important to build these collaborative relationships and partnerships?
- What role did you play?
- Who was involved?
- How did you obtain credibility and trust as a collaborator and partner?

- How did you influence key stakeholders—senior management, peer groups, your team, external stakeholders, and others—to work together as collaborative partners?
- What actions did you take to ensure success?
- What obstacles did you face?
- What actions did you take to overcome them?
- What was the outcome?

3. Now reflect on a time when you contributed as an influential team member in leading and managing a significant change.

- What was the context (internal and external, global and local) that influenced your work?
- What was your role and contribution?
- When were you successful and why?
- When were you challenged and why?
- What did you learn about yourself that you keep top of mind as you lead meaningful change?

4. What are your overall reflections on leading meaningful change?
- What are the key themes and patterns that you have observed about yourself?
- What are your strengths as a leader?
- Where are you most challenged?

→ Part 2: Change Leadership Competencies Self-Assessment

Using the results of the above assessment, complete the following change leadership competencies self-assessment. You can use this self-assessment as a baseline to monitor how well you are doing individually and as a team throughout the change process.

Step 1
For each question, use the scale 1 = no agreement to 8 = full agreement to best indicate your status.

1 = no agreement 8 = full agreement	1	2	3	4	5	6	7	8
1. I understand the vision, direction, and context for leading the changes.								
2. I have strategies to lead the change in my department.								
3. I have strategies to lead the change with key stakeholders outside my department.								
4. I am confident in my ability to lead the change across the organization.								
5. I understand my role in leading the change.								
6. I am effective developing and implementing strategies to help people overcome resistance and adapt to the change.								
7. I am effective working on the leadership team to lead change.								
8. I am effective working with my management team to lead change.								
9. I am effective working on the project team to lead change.								
10. I am effective building collaborative relationships to lead and implement the change plan.								
11. I am effective communicating change.								
12. I am effective engaging my staff in the change process.								
13. I am effective developing, coaching, and mentoring others.								
14. I am achieving my goals and objectives in leading this change.								
15. I have effective practices, tools, and support for my own learning and development.								
16. I am fully engaged in the change process.								

Step 2

Answer these questions:

1. What are the top three priorities that will help you to successfully lead change?
2. What do you expect to achieve by working on these priorities?
3. What actions will you take to achieve your objectives?
4. How will you measure success?

Assessing Your Personal Style of Managing Exercise

→ Step 1: Self-Assessment

Consider how you manage in your job. Circle one of the three words in each row that best describes your style. When you are finished, add up how many you have circled in each of the three columns. Together they should add up to ten.

Ideas	Experiences	Facts
Intuitive	Practical	Analytical
Heart	Hands-on	Head
Strategies	Processes	Outcomes
Inspiring	Engaging	Informing
Passionate	Helpful	Reliable
Novel	Realistic	Determined
Imagining	Learning	Organizing
Seeing it	Doing it	Thinking it
"The possibilities are endless!"	"Consider it done!"	"That's perfect!"
Total scores		

→ **Step 2: Review Your Results and the Theory**

The first column represents art, the second craft, and the third science. This assessment was developed by Beverley Patwell and Henry Mintzberg in 2008, based on the work of Henry Mintzberg and described in his books *Managing* (2009) and *Simply Managing* (2013).[25]

These three styles—art, craft, and science—are highlighted in the triangle shown below.

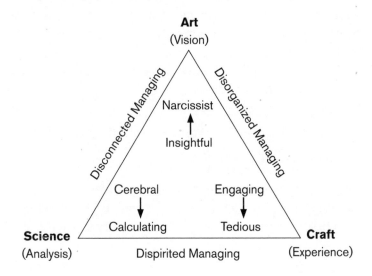

- Close to science is the cerebral style—deliberate and analytical.
- Close to art is the insightful style—concerned with ideas and vision and intuitive in nature.
- Close to craft is an engaging style—hands-on, helpful, and rooted in experience.

Excessive attention to any one of these styles can lead to imbalanced managing.

The cerebral style can become *calculating*, placing too much emphasis on science and analysis. The insightful style can become *narcissistic*, paying too much attention to art.

The engaging style can become *tedious*, hesitating to venture beyond the manager's own experience.

Even a combination of two of these styles without the third can be problematic, as shown on the three lines of the triangle: a disorganized style (no science), a disconnected style (no craft), and a dispiriting style (no art).

Effective managing requires a blend of art, craft, and science, whether in the person of the manager alone or in a management team that works together. Management may not be a science, but it does need some of the order of science while being rooted in the practicality of craft, with the zest of art.

→ Step 3: Complete These Reflection Questions on Your Own or as a Team

1. What is your preferred approach to managing?
2. What effect does your style have on your ability to lead meaningful change?
3. What are your strengths?
4. What are your development opportunities?
5. Review your results and insights from this assessment with your development plan and identify any actions you want to add or enhance in your plan.

Leading Meaningful Change Self-Development Guide

Leading meaningful change can be a time of great excitement and opportunity. For others, it can also be a challenging time—one of loss, confusion, and uncertainty. This self-development guide is designed to support you and your team by

- creating a shared understanding of the plan;
- deepening your understanding of your roles and responsibilities and how you will work together as a cohesive team;

- creating alignment and an action plan to communicate about your way forward; and
- providing content, tools, and resources to continue to develop your ability to lead and manage the changes required for success.

This exercise is designed to help you reflect on your critical role as a member of the leadership team and as the leader of your change project initiative, branch, department, or service area. It is also designed to help you develop your own personal leadership development plan to support your learning and growth throughout the change process and advance your real work in leading and managing meaningful change.

→ Step 1

The following process is designed to help you initiate your personal development plan:

1. Review your project and/or change initiative priorities.
2. Review your role, mandate, and organizational structure.
3. Review your team's priorities.
4. Review any feedback that you may have received.

→ Step 2

Throughout the process, people will be looking to you for leadership, inspiration, and confidence. You will also need to engage them to follow and embrace the new strategy and direction for your organization. The following questions are designed to help you develop some key messages for your staff, family, and colleagues about your leadership philosophy and purpose.

Vision and Purpose

- What is your personal vision and purpose?
- Why do you want to be a leader at this time of the organization's history?
- What do you aspire to achieve as a leader and a member of the leadership or project team?
- How will you know you are successful in your role?
- What professional and personal development or life and work experiences have prepared you for this role?
- What successes or accomplishments are you most proud of so far?
- Why are these accomplishments so meaningful for you?

Values

- What values guide your work and are these values in alignment with the leadership team's values?
- How do you bring these values to life in your daily work? Which ones do you have the hardest time keeping?
- What strategies can you put in place to ensure you stay true to your values?
- What behaviors must you exhibit to your department and the organization to demonstrate that you are living the shared values of the leadership team?

Priorities

- What are your top priorities?
- Given what you know about your branch, department, or service area, the leadership team's priorities, and your role in supporting the changes, what are the most important issues that you need to address as a leader and as a member of the leadership team to make a difference and ensure success?
- What do you think the leadership team must collectively address?

- Think about what the benefits will be for various stakeholders, including yourself, the leadership team, your branch, your department, your service area, the community, your industry, and others.

Development and Support Plan

- What development and supports do you need to be successful?

To help you answer this question, you may want to review previous leadership assessments, 360-degree feedback results, performance reviews, employee satisfaction surveys, and any other forms of feedback that you might have received over the last few years to reflect on what you know about yourself.

You might also want to review your role and mandate as a leader and member of the team. Reflect on where you are comfortable and where you might be stretched or developing.

Here are a few questions to help you consider what you might also be thinking and/or feeling about your personal leadership journey:

- What changes, both personal and professional, do you foresee as a result of taking on this change, your new role, or the new direction?
- What are you excited about?
- What are your worries, fears, and concerns?
- What strengths will you leverage?
- What do you need to let go of to fully embrace this change?
- What obstacles do you need to overcome to achieve your goals?
- What relationships with your colleagues on the team do you need to focus on building or nurturing for success?
- What supports and development do you and your team need to successfully work with the following stakeholders?

	Yourself	Your Team
Executive, senior management team		
Direct reports		
Peers		
Project teams		
Employees		
Clients, customers		
Governing boards, committees		
External political stakeholders		
External industry stakeholders		
Community partners		
Others		

Development Goals

Based on your personal leadership assessment:

- What are your hopes, wishes, and expectations?
- What personal, departmental, or organizational goals do you want to achieve in the next one to two years?
- How will you measure success?

Given the answers to these questions, develop two to three development goals that you will work on over the next 6 to 12 months. Here is a guide to write your goal and a sample to help you get started.

"In the next 6 to 12 months, I will (describe the goal and actions...) so that (describe the benefit for yourself and others). Indicators of my progress will be (describe the results that you and others will see)."

SAMPLE GOAL STATEMENT

In the next 6 to 12 months, I will communicate my vision and values for leading and implementing a plan to create a shared purpose throughout the organization. I will implement the process consistently and in a compelling manner so that my management team and all of my staff will be inspired, be engaged, and be able to clearly articulate how they support a shared vision for our branch, department, or service area. Indicators of my progress will be direct feedback on how well I am communicating our shared vision and the plan from my managers and staff. I will also hear from them about how they are demonstrating the mindset, values, and behaviors of the vision and their accomplishments.

Support Systems

The following is a guide developed by Charlie Seashore, who defined a support system as "a resource pool, drawn on selectively, to support me in moving in a direction of my choice, which leaves me stronger."[26] As you develop your support system, think about the following:

1. What am I experiencing?
2. What type of support do I need?
3. How will this support help me?

Think about what resources you have in your network to support your learning and development. What types of internal and external supports do you need to continue, nurture, or develop? Ensure your support system includes people who will challenge you, support you, develop you, and hold you accountable to your plan.

Experience	Support Type	Outcomes
Confusion	Role models, mentors, and coaches	Clarity
Isolation	People with common interests	Social-professional contacts
Vulnerability	Helpers-experts	Supported
Lack of confidence	Affirmation of my strengths	Confidence
Disconnection	Referrals	Connections
Plateau	Challengers	Cutting edge

→ Step 3

Now fill out the template below and share your plan with your boss or the person whom you selected to hold you accountable.

Leadership Development Plan
Vision and Purpose
Values
Priorities

What are your top three development priorities?	Why is this priority important?	What impact are you hoping to achieve for yourself and others?
1.		
2.		
3.		

Development and Support Plan

What strengths will you leverage?	What opportunities will you embrace for development?

Goal Statement

Actions What actions will you take to achieve your goals?	Expected Outcomes How will you measure success?	Date

Accountability Who can you enlist to hold you accountable for following through on your development plan?		Support System Who will you seek out for support?

Endnotes

[1] Becky May and Kim Seashore, "From the Daughters of Edie and Charlie Seashore, Becky and Kim." *Organizational Development Journal. Part 2: Self as Instrument. A Tribute to Charlie and Edie Seashore* 37, no. 2 (Summer 2019): 9.

[2] The term "Use-of-Self" is considered to have first appeared in the book *Education through Recreation*, written in the 1930s by Lawrence Pearsall Jacks, a Unitarian minister.

[3] Charles N. Seashore, foreword to *Triple Impact Coaching: Use-of-Self in the Coaching Process*, by Beverley Patwell and Edith Whitfield Seashore (Victoria, BC: Patwell Consulting Inc., 2006), 8.

[4] Charles N. Seashore, Mary Nash Shawver, Greg Thompson, and Marty Mattare, "Doing Good by Knowing Who You Are: The Instrumental Self as an Agent of Change," *OD Practitioner* 36, no. 3 (2004): 57.

[5] Mary Ann Rainey and Brenda B. Jones, "Use-of-Self: Presence with the Power to Transform Systems," *Organizational Development Journal* 37, no. 2 (Summer 2019): 11, 13.

[6] Henry Mintzberg, *Managing* (San Francisco: Berrett-Koehler Publishers, 2009), 37–38.

7 Beverley Patwell, *Triple Impact Coaching: Use-of-Self in the Coaching Process: Reflecting on the Past, Present, and Future*, *Organizational Development Journal* (Summer 2019): 1–12.

8 Chris Musselwhite and Randell Jones, *Dangerous Opportunity: Making Change Work*, 2nd ed. (Greensboro, NC: Discovery Learning Inc., 2010), 137.

9 Stephanie Jones and Jonathan Gosling, *Napoleonic Leadership: A Study in Power* (Thousand Oaks, CA: Sage Publications, 2015), 136.

10 Dan Pontefract, *The Purpose Effect: Building Meaning in Yourself, Your Role, and Your Organization* (Vancouver: Figure 1 Publishing, 2016).

11 Colin Hall and Caitlin Comeau, *Informal Learning: A Spotlight on Hidden Learning in the Canadian Workplace* (Conference Board of Canada, August 2018), https://www.conferenceboard.ca/e-library/abstract.aspx?did=9861.

12 Todd Armstrong and Ruth Wright, *Employee Engagement: Leveraging the Science to Inspire Great Performance* (Conference Board of Canada, July 2016), https://www.conferenceboard.ca/e-library/abstract.aspx?did=7924.

13 Henry Mintzberg, *Rebalancing Society: Radical Renewal Beyond Left, Right, and Center* (Oakland: Berrett-Koehler Publishers, 2015); *Rebalancing Society: Starting Now* (CoachingOurselves module, 2019), www.coachingourselves.com.

14 McKinsey & Company, *The Science of Organizational Transformations* (September 2015), https://www.mckinsey.com/business-functions/organization/our-insights/the-science-of-organizational-transformations.

15 Edgar Schein, *Probing into Culture* (CoachingOurselves module, 2010), 5, www.coachingourselves.com.

16 Edgar Schein, *The Corporate Culture Survival Guide, New and Revised Edition* (San Francisco: Jossey-Bass, 2009).

[17] Beverley Patwell, Donna Gray, and Steve Kanellakos, "Discovering the Magic of Culture Shifts: A Case Study in Large Scale Culture Transformation," *OD Practitioner* 44, no. 1 (2012): 14.

[18] Beverley Patwell, "Leadership Sustainability: A Framework to Sustain Culture Shifts," Queen's University IRC (2014): 4, https://irc.queensu.ca/articles/leadership-sustainability-framework-sustain-culture-shifts.

[19] Beverley Patwell, Christina Bruce, Leah Zilnik, and Laura Mirabella-Siddall, "The Stewardship of Service Excellence at the City of Vaughan: Reflections on Sustaining Momentum, Building Capacity and Focus during Transformational Change," Queen's University IRC (2016), https://irc.queensu.ca/articles/stewardship-service-excellence-city-vaughan.

[20] Patrick Lencioni, *Overcoming the Five Dysfunctions of a Team: A Field Guide for Leaders, Managers, and Facilitators* (San Francisco: Jossey-Bass, 2005), 6.

[21] Patwell, Gray, and Kanellakos, "Discovering the Magic of Culture Shifts."

[22] James W. Sipe and Don M. Frick, *Seven Pillars of Servant Leadership: Practicing the Wisdom of Leading by Serving,* 2nd ed. (New York: Paulist Press, 2015).

[23] Additional resources about this City of Ottawa case study include *Leading Transitions Handbook: Leadership, Alignment, Teamwork and Collaboration*, internal document (2016); "City Manager and Administration," https://ottawa.ca/en/city-hall/city-manager-and-administration; and the internal documents "City Manager Message," "Frequently Asked Questions," and "Backgrounder," stored on the City of Ottawa's intranet.

[24] Sipe and Frick, *Seven Pillars of Servant Leadership*.

[25] Henry Mintzberg, *Simply Managing: What Managers Do—and Can Do Better* (San Francisco: Berrett-Koehler Publishers, 2013), 87. See also note 6.

[26] In Patwell and Seashore, *Triple Impact Coaching*, 101.

Acknowledgments

I stand on the shoulders of many people who have influenced and supported me in my life's work. They are my teachers, mentors, coaches, clients, colleagues, collaborators, partners, advisors, family, and friends. I would like to thank all of you for your contribution to my learning, growth, and development.

I would like to acknowledge the people who helped me in a major way with the ideas and content that shaped the development of Leading Meaningful Change and this book.

First, I want to acknowledge Charlie and Edie Seashore, who introduced me to the concept of Use-of-Self. Although they are no longer with us, I know they were alongside me as I wrote this book. Their legacy lives on.

I want to acknowledge the people at the City of Ottawa for their support of my work over many years and their significant contributions to this approach. I especially want to acknowledge Steve Kanellakos for his quote: "When you are successful leading meaningful change, it means that you have captured the hearts and souls of the people. They believe in a higher purpose, something greater than their own single contribution." This quote was the inspiration for the title and framing of the book.

I also want to thank Donna Gray, an exceptional transformation leader. She has been alongside me from the very beginning. I am so grateful for her sage advice and the many opportunities that we have had to collaborate and co-create together.

I want to acknowledge the hard work, dedication, and commitment of the senior leadership team. They are exceptional servant leaders. I am deeply honored to have had the opportunity to work with you and to learn from each and every one of you. Thank you for your personal and team contributions to the case study. My heartfelt thanks to Steve, Donna, Tony Di Monte, John Manconi, Steve Box, Kevin Wylie, John Moser, Janice Burelle, Marian Simulik, Dan Chenier, Rick O'Connor, and Steve Willis. A special thank-you to Deirdre Luesby and her design teams for their help in developing, facilitating, and supporting the processes, tools, and supports for the transition and transformation process.

I also want to thank Dora Koop and Henry Mintzberg from McGill University's Desautels Faculty of Management for inviting me to pilot the Advanced Leadership Program so many years ago. This experience was life-changing for me. Henry, thank you for sharing your wisdom and for the many opportunities that we have had to collaborate, partner, and work together.

I want to acknowledge the CoachingOurselves network and especially Henry Mintzberg and Phil LeNir for your coaching and efforts to provide tools and supports to help us rebalance society by reflecting and learning with and from each other, inside our organizations and beyond. Thank you Jonathan Gosling for your study on Napoleonic leadership, which is so relevant for helping us navigate the power dynamics at play in our world today.

I have also walked alongside extraordinary people who have been part of this incredible journey of leading meaningful change. This book is based on the real stories and experiences of my clients, participants in workshops, students, and colleagues. Without them, this book would not exist. I am grateful to all of you for your inspiration, participation, and contributions that have shaped this LMC approach.

I have also worked with many partners who have promoted and supported change and transformation programs. Paul Slaggert and the team at the Stayer Center for Executive Education at Mendoza College of Business, University of Notre Dame, thank you for taking a chance on this Canadian and for supporting our Change Leadership Essentials and ExperienceChange workshops for more than a decade. It has been a great honor to work with you and the team.

I also want to thank Paul Juniper, Stephanie Noël, and the Queen's University IRC team for your support of our Designing Change programs and for publishing the articles that tell the stories that have shaped this approach.

My thanks also go to Sandra Nichol, Kevin Caron, Dr. William Taylor, and the team at Concordia University's John Molson School of Business for your support and for championing our programs, specifically the Airports Council International (ACI) Airport Executive Leadership Programme and the International Civil Aviation Organization (ICAO) Certificate in Human Resources Management Program. It is always a thrill to go back to my home base and teach. Thank you to Dr. Raye Kass for teaching me the foundations of interpersonal dynamics and group development, which continue to be critical to my work.

One of the key elements and foundations of my work is the ExperienceChange simulation created by James Chisholm and Greg Warman of ExperiencePoint. I have been using this simulation with clients all over the world for almost 20 years. We've had a great time learning about change and, at the same time, developing meaningful strategies that have helped to change the world. I also want to thank the incredible technical support team at ExperiencePoint who for years have been in the background making sure there are no hiccups with the technology. Thank you for your support. You are amazing!

Thank you to the networks that I have been a part of and who have influenced my thinking and provided me with exceptional professional development, wise practices, and a rich learning network: the Niagara Institute (Conference Board of Canada), Discovery Learning, National Training Laboratories, the Organization Development Network, and the Lewin Center.

I would like to thank Roland Livingston for the invitation to write an article for the special edition of the International Society for Organization Development and Change's tribute to Charlie and Edie Seashore, which was the catalyst for the study *Triple Impact Coaching: Use-of-Self in the Coaching Process: Reflecting on the Past, Present, and Future*; Katherine Farquhar for her sage advice and coaching; and Brenda B. Jones and Mary Ann Rainey for sharing their Four Elements of Self Framework. I know the Seashores would be honored.

I would also like to thank Glennie Goins of Discovery Learning for administering the Change Style Indicator assessments for our programs all over the world.

Thank you to the many people who participated in the *Change Leadership Challenges* and *Triple Impact Coaching* studies. There are too many of you to mention personally, but you have my deepest gratitude.

Thank you to Dr. Cynthia Smith and the School of Health and Human Services leadership group at Camosun College for embracing the CoachingOurselves process and sharing your case study.

Thank you to the publishing team at Figure 1 for your expertise and support throughout the journey of writing this book. I want to especially acknowledge Rick Benzel, the master editor, for his invaluable contribution in helping me bring to life my vision for this book. I really could not have done this without you. I am grateful for your patience, coaching, and all your questions that helped me bring out my voice and be focused and clear.

I also want to thank Charles Raywood and Steve Walters from Profile Direct Marketing. We have worked together for over 20 years. Thank you for the images and graphics. Steve, a special thank-you for sharing your pantomime story.

Pauline Conley, thank you for developing the LMC imagery that inspired the LMC model.

I also want to thank my colleagues who read the drafts of the book and provided me with rich and valuable feedback. Ross Roxburgh, who asked me the question, "Bev, what are you going to do to celebrate the tenth anniversary of Triple Impact?": who knew this would be the answer? Thank you, Ross, and thank you Jenny Sardone and Glenda Pryce.

This work could not have been done without my personal support system who fed and nourished me as I did my work in Ottawa and Montreal. I want to thank Darla Shaw, Harry Meredith, Diana Haddad, Wanda Hoskin, Monique Marsan, Lynne Gervais, Jean Luk Pellerin, and my family and friends.

Lastly, and most importantly, I am ever so grateful to my husband, Don, for his unwavering support and belief in me. This book was a journey for both of us. It took more time than was planned, but he was there for me every step of the way. Yes, even as my IT guy and office manager. Every time I wanted to take a short cut, he encouraged me to pause, catch my breath, and remember the importance of this book. Don, you captured my heart and bring meaning to my life.

Index

*Tables, figures, and checklists
indicated by page numbers in italics*

Beverley Patwell is the president and founder of Patwell Consulting Inc. Her focus for over 30 years has been on helping people learn about, lead, and achieve meaningful change and transformation in their lives, at work, and in organizations and communities.

Her approach to change has been used by individuals, teams, and organizations around the world in the private, public, and plural sectors.

Beverley is a consultant, coach, professor, and academic-practitioner who specializes in leadership, coaching, organizational development, and change. She is the recipient of the International Coach Federation's Prism Award for Executive Coaching.

In addition to her consulting work, she serves as a professor at the University of Notre Dame, Queen's University, and Concordia University, where she teaches courses on leading change. She is a partner with CoachingOurselves and a facilitation partner with ExperiencePoint.

Beverley is the co-author with Edith Whitfield Seashore of *Triple Impact Coaching: Use-of-Self in the Coaching Process* and the CoachingOurselves topic *Coaching Others*. She has also written numerous professional articles on leadership, coaching, and transformation that have been published in the *Organizational Development Journal* (ISODC), Queen's University IRC publications, and other journals.

Beverley was born in Montreal, Quebec, and now resides in Victoria, British Columbia, with her husband, Don.

Further information about Patwell Consulting can be found at www.patwellconsulting.com. Beverley can be contacted at bpatwell@patwellconsulting.com.

20 21 22 23 24   5 4 3 2 1

Cataloguing data are available from Library and Archives Canada
ISBN 978-1-77327-085-2 (pbk.)
ISBN 978-1-77327-101-9 (ebook)
ISBN 978-1-77327-102-6 (pdf)

Cover design by Naomi MacDougall
Interior design by Gerilee McBride
Editing by Rick Benzel
Copy editing by Lana Okerlund
Proofreading by Alison Strobel
Indexing by Stephen Ullstrom
Author photograph by Don Boyd

Printed and bound in Canada by Friesens
Distributed internationally by Publishers Group West

Figure 1 Publishing Inc.
Vancouver BC Canada
www.figure1publishing.com